BASIC ASTROLOGY
A GUIDE FOR TEACHERS & STUDENTS

JOAN NEGUS

Published by
ACS Publications, Inc.
P.O. Box 16430
San Diego, California 92116

International Standard Book Number 0-917086-14-7

Published by ACS Publications, Inc.
P.O. Box 16430
San Diego, CA 92116

Printed in the United States of America

First printing, June 1978
Second printing, December 1982
Third printing, March 1987

Dedication

To Ken, my husband and teacher, without whom I would not have become an astrologer.

Acknowledgements

My thanks to Neil Michelsen for inviting me to write this book, which had been forming in my mind for so long. My thanks to Nona Press for her superb editing job. My thanks finally to my students who helped me crystallize many ideas, and particularly to those who have gone on to teach.

CONTENTS

INTRODUCTION

The goal of a basic astrology course is not only to teach the fundamentals but also to help the student develop the insight and logic needed to interpret a chart. Anyone can learn key words and definitions, and memorization is important in the early stages of studying the subject; but integration of the material is essential.

The logic and cohesiveness of the system should be stressed by relating each area presented to other areas already covered. Key words should be kept to a minimum and interrelationships used to trigger the mind to further meanings. The creative thinking process is thus begun early in the course, with the teacher setting the limits so that the imagination does not drift into illogical directions.

As each part is presented, it should be related not only to the other parts, but also to knowledge the student already has on the other subjects. The hemisphere emphasis is described first because everyone has read a map or looked at a globe, and it is less difficult to adjust to the reversal of directions (astrologers placing south at the top of the chart) than to totally new concepts. In the hemisphere emphasis the student is exposed to the MC-IC, Ascendant-Descendant, and the glyphs of the planets before he is asked to understand the meanings of the points and planets.

Marc Edmund Jones' temperament patterns are introduced next to expand the meaning of the hemisphere emphasis and to begin the integration process. The temperament patterns are used because they provide a visual as well as a verbal aid—a picture of the chart as a whole. As explained on the temperament pattern definition sheets, one rarely finds a chart that is a perfect example of any of the patterns and, therefore, definitions have to be blended. As astrological knowledge and skills are developed, the patterns may be modified or altered; but in the beginning it is important to keep concepts as simple and concrete as possible. Jones' concepts are relatively easy to understand in terms of experience outside of astrology (seesaw triggers the idea of balance; splash, diversification, etc.).

The next few lessons are devoted to the thirty-four primary factors—the twelve houses, ten planets and twelve signs. It is clearly explained that the houses represent departments or compartments of life; planets, functions; and signs, characteristics, so that the factors can be distinguished from each other and later combined in a meaningful way.

With the presentation of the thirty-four primary factors the memorization process must begin, but this process can be aided by keeping definitions simple, by interrelating the factors and by relating factors to information the student may already possess. The houses are described first because their meanings are less complex than those of planets and signs, and because one is relating an area of the chart to an area of life. The planets are presented next. Besides giving positive and negative key words, the teacher should also utilize the physical properties of the planets and mythological correlations where possible. These analogies assist in the memorization process. For example, the Sun shines and is visible, and therefore it is easy to remember that the Sun is the part of the personality that "shines." The elements, modes and polarity are explained and related to the signs as the signs are introduced. The houses and planets are also integrated with the signs. The student is then beginning to get a coherent picture of the basics of astrology and discovering that each part helps him to better understand the other parts.

Aspects are added next. First, the meanings of the individual aspects are given and then combined to reveal major configurations which indicate basic patterns in the native's life. The elements, modes, houses, planets and signs are integrated into the patterns.

The student then is ready to begin to synthesize. A work sheet, which incorporates everything learned thus far and organizes the material, is studied very carefully. A step-by-step method of interpretation follows. Every new chart will help to expand the student's knowledge.

In synthesizing, and in each step leading to it, the holistic and therapeutic approach is taken. The essence of the chart is more important than concentrating on a single planet or aspect, or house or sign. Deep analysis or dissection of the chart should be undertaken only after the whole person is grasped, otherwise one could distort the total picture of the individual by focusing on an area which is only a small part of the life. The approach is therapeutic in that the purpose in studying the chart is to promote self-understanding, to realize potential and to develop a sense of wholeness of self. The holistic viewing of the chart comes about quite naturally by integrating the parts of astrology as they are studied. By teaching the desirable and undesirable manifestations of planets, signs and aspects, and showing how both the desirable and the undersirable work, one points up that there are choices which can be made; that some degree of free will exists; and that there is a therapeutic value to astrology.

There are two suggestions which if followed can contribute to the success of this method. One is that homework assignments be given to help reinforce what is being taught in class, to encourage the student to contribute to the class as the homework is reviewed, and eventually to enable him to work independently. *Basic Astrology: A Workbook for Students* is designed to facilitate this process. The combination of this book and the Workbook provides the most efficient way to utilize the materials. The text provides a succinct, cohesive method of teaching for learning astrology, and the Workbook contains the parts that reinforce the memorization and understanding of the subject.

All of the homework sheets, charts and other materials from this book which are essential to the students have been combined in the Workbook. The homework is presented without answers (available in the text) to help the student avoid the temptation to "peek." If each student has a copy of this Workbook the learning process is made easier because the papers are ordered according to course sequence and the teachers is relieved of the chore of reproducing the materials. Students also grasp what is being taught in class more quickly when they have pertinent information to reinforce class lectures and for reference afterwards.

Students seem to agree that the assignments are fun, give them a feeling of accomplishment and make the principles of astrology relatively simple to learn.

The other suggestion is that classes be kept small so that all students can be drawn into class discussions and interpretations. It is extremely important that the students verbalize what they are learning. In this way they reinforce their own understanding; and when all students are contributing to the class, the learning process becomes a lively and interesting joint effort.

The role of the teacher is to present the materials, set the guidelines for the interpretation and to form the class into a working unit.

This course includes widely accepted astrological concepts which can be found in a variety of introductory texts. It is the *framework* that is unique to this text, but the framework is flexible enough to accommodate the individual teacher's ideas within each area. The definitions are those favored by the writer but kept simple in the hope that the teacher using the method, as well as the student, will use the materials creatively. The method has been designed primarily for the teacher of astrology, but it can be of benefit to the student who wishes to teach himself.

1

HEMISPHERE EMPHASIS & TEMPERAMENT PATTERNS

If the class is begun with the question "What do you think astrology is?", class participation starts immediately.

This leads to a definition by the teacher. The teacher's definition should include the information that scientific data (astronomical positions of planets and precise mathematical information) are employed and interpreted in their relevance to human affairs.

Why does astrology work? There seems to be a correlation or correspondence between the movement of the universe and life on earth, and there are a number of theories as to why. One source in which these theories are explained is *The Case for Astrology* by John Anthony West and Jan Gerhard Toonder (Coward-McCann, Inc., New York, 1970, p. 214 f.)

How does astrology work? In basic astrology we utilize the signs of the Zodiac; the planets (those which have been sighted, minus the earth, plus the Sun and our Moon—which are called "planets" in astrology for convenience); and a division of the zodiac into houses. These factors are combined to form the horoscope, which is a picture of the sky at a given moment in a given location.

At the center of the horoscope is the earth. Astrologers know that the earth revolves around the Sun, but we are interested in the relationship of the planets to the earth, since we are investigating life on earth.

The most important circle with which we deal in a horoscope is the apparent path of the Sun around the earth, called the ecliptic. The picture presented by a horoscope is roughly that of a person standing at a given geographical location and facing south (but aware of what is behind him and beneath his feet), thus making the ecliptic visible to him in the southern part of the sky. This causes the directions to be the reverse of those on a map. We are looking at the *earth* to read a map but at the *sky* to read a horoscope.

The planets are never far from the ecliptic, so they are positioned on a circle of the horoscope.

In tropical astrology the signs are formed by the position of the Sun in relationship to the earth. When the Sun is directly over the equator at the Vernal Equinox, it is at the zero Aries point. When the Sun is at its northernmost position at the Summer Solstice, it is at the zero Cancer point. When the Sun, after the Summer Solstice, is again at a position directly over the equator, it is at the Autumnal Equinox point at zero degrees Libra. When the Sun is at its southernmost position at the Winter Solstice, it is at zero Capricorn. These four points are the cardinal points and form quadrants on the ecliptic. Each quadrant is further divided into thirds, and this gives us the twelve signs of the Zodiac.

The houses are based on the exact position of a point on the earth in the earth's daily twenty-four-hour rotation. (This especially makes the time and location of birth important.) The point due south on the ecliptic (overhead) at the moment of birth is the MC or Midheaven; and the point on the eastern horizon at the latitude of birth becomes the Ascendant. These points are the same in most of the various house systems, but otherwise the division into houses varies.

A combination of planets, signs and houses—as described above—forms the horoscope, which is the basic tool of astrology. How do we use it?

The factors in a horoscope represent everything conceivable in human life. The houses divide life into departments or compartments (the fourth house represents, among other things, the area or compartment of the more closely linked parent). The planets designate functions (the Moon represents, among other things, the maternal function). The signs embody characteristics (Cancer represents motherliness, protectiveness, etc.).

Each factor is multileveled so that one can investigate the physical, the psychological or the spiritual implications of any given factor.

In this course each of the levels will be investigated. The goal of the course is to help the student better understand himself and others, and to provide a structure through which one can work toward the integration of separate parts and a sense of wholeness.

The basic concepts of astrology will be taught, as well as the casting of a horoscope. Teaching is a joint effort, so the student must participate by memorizing as homework the glyphs and meanings introduced in class. Before the memorization begins, however, one can start to interpret a chart by mere placement of planets without regard to specific houses or signs or meanings of planets. This is called hemisphere emphasis.

For hemisphere emphasis take the circle of the horoscope and divide it in half horizontally, and then vertically. The vertical axis is called the MC-IC axis. Everything to the left of this axis is eastern; if a majority of the planets are positioned there, this is one indication that the individual is an initiator. Everything to the right of this axis is western; if a majority of the planets are positioned there, this is one indication that the individual is a responder. The horizontal axis is called the Ascendant-Descendant axis. Everything above this axis is southern; if a majority of the planets are positioned there, this is one indication that the individual primarily adjusts to the world. Everything below this axis is northern; if a majority of the planets are positioned there, this is one indication that the individual basically adjusts the world to him.

7

Hemisphere Emphasis

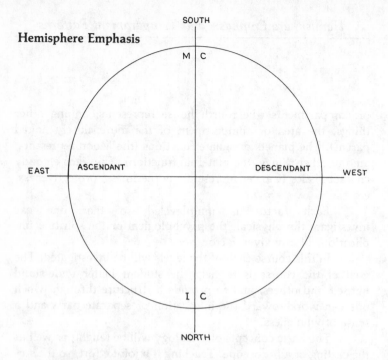

More information can be added by the introduction of visual patterns.* By combining the hemisphere definitions with the meanings of the overall patterns, the chart synthesis is begun, and with it comes a more general understanding of the individual being studied. A chart for each Temperament Pattern is presented. As the students look at each chart, the teacher should read each definition. The class together can count the planets by hemisphere and add this tally to the pattern interpretation. (For example, Theodore Roosevelt is the example of the Splash, meaning that he had a wide variety of interests and in his case was the "universal" man. He has six planets in the east and four in the west—a little more an initiator than a responder. He has five planets in the north and five in the south—equally adjusting to the world and adjusting the world to him. There are many examples in his life that support this description.) At this point, homework should be assigned.

---

*The basic categories were taken from *The Guide to Horoscope Interpretation* by Marc Edmund Jones, Sabian Publishing Society: Stanwood, Washington, 1967. See also Jones' *Essentials of Astrological Analysis, 1960.*

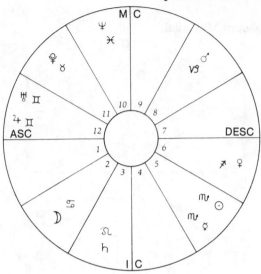

Temperament Patterns

The temperament patterns are used primarily as a visual approach to synthesis. The title of each pattern should trigger a plausible meaning for the positioning of planets in that pattern. Rarely will the patterns be found in charts in their ideal form. It is necessary, therefore, that the student find the one which is closest to the ideal; or if parts of two or more patterns seem to be indicated, these patterns should be blended together in the interpretation.

As the chart is more deeply analyzed, the patterns may be modified in the light of other evidence; but the purpose of the patterns is to establish a general quality in the chart, so that one can begin to interpret holistically rather than in a fragmented way.

Splash (an image of "scatteredness"). In the splash pattern the planets are in eight to ten different signs or houses. At best it indicates the universal man, interested in many things and knowing many of them well. At worst it is the jack-of-all-trades and master-of-none.

Bundle:Benito Mussolini

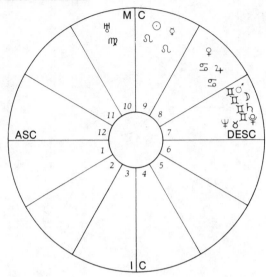

     Bundle (an image of things bound closely together). In the Bundle pattern all the planets are within a trine (120º). This denotes an individual who has very narrow interests. Hemisphere emphasis individualizes the Bundle. A predominantly northeastern Bundle shows a person who is self-sufficient and adjusts the world to himself. A northwestern Bundle shows a person whose opportunities come from others, but then he adapts situations to himself.

     A southeastern Bundle is indicative of an individual who initiates, but in terms of adjusting to the world. A southwestern Bundle is reflective of a person who adjusts to the world, trying to do what is expected of him. His opportunities come from others. It is possible that the Bundle will not be entirely within one quadrant, and, therefore, the above definitions would have to be combined.

     Locomotive (an image of hard-driving, forward action). In this pattern there is an empty trine (120º). All the planets are within 240º, with no more than a sextile (60º) from one to the

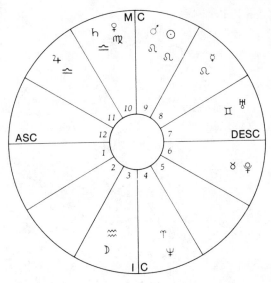

next. An individual with a Locomotive pattern tends to be self-driving and dynamic. He can be a pioneer in some area.

  Bowl (the image of a container which holds liquid that is poured into it, the liquid taking on the shape of the container). In this configuration all of the planets are within one opposition (180°) and ideally are in six signs or houses. A person with a bowl pattern is self-contained and develops mainly through experience (as experience pours in, it takes on the shape of the individual). Hemisphere emphasis determines whether the individual keeps his development within himself (northern) or shares it with the world (southern); or if he initiates his experience (eastern), or if opportunities come from others for his experience (western). The Bowl will include at least two quadrants; therefore the hemisphere emphasis will be blended into the pattern interpretation.

  Bucket (the image of a container with a handle). In the Bucket pattern, ideally nine planets are in one half of the chart within 180°, and one planet is in the opposite half of the chart

Bowl:Helen Keller

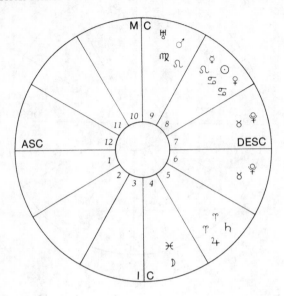

opposing the nine. Or eight planets may be in one half of the chart within 180°, with two planets in conjunction opposing the eight. The eight or nine planets which are together form a "bowl," so that the definition of the Bucket also includes self-containment and development through experience. The one or two planets forming the "handle" add another element, however. This planet or these planets provide a point of release for the energy of the native. He must, in some way, give back to the world what he has experienced in the world, even if the native is primarily northern.

There is a variation of the Bucket, whereby the eight or nine planets are within a trine (120°) resembling a Bundle rather than a Bowl. This variation signifies that this individual has narrower interests than the person with a Bowl. The handle still represents a point of release for the energy of the native. This pattern is called a "Bundle-Bucket."

12

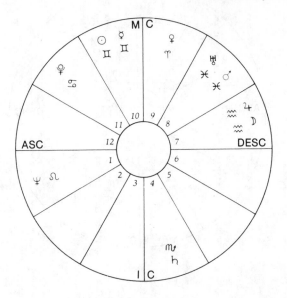

Seesaw (the image of a seesaw going up and down and connoting balance). In the seesaw pattern the planets fall in opposition to each other. Ideally, five planets oppose five others. It may be, however, that as many as seven planets will oppose three others. This configuration shows a need for the native to balance different areas and energies in his life, or the effect will be separative.What particularly must be balanced depends on the planets themselves, the signs and the houses involved.

Splay (an image of a wheel with several spokes, not necessarily evenly spaced but holding the wheel together). In the Splay the planets fall into three, four or five groups, each usually involving a conjunction. Each spoke indicates an area of interest. A person with a splay configuration is usually an individualist. His interests will be few (generally as many as he has spokes), but these will be highly developed. He will delve deeply into whatever interests him.

13

Seesaw:Richard Nixon

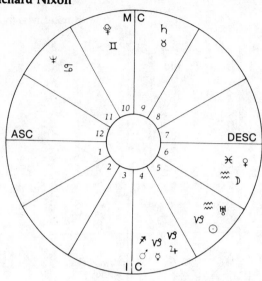

Splay:Babe Ruth

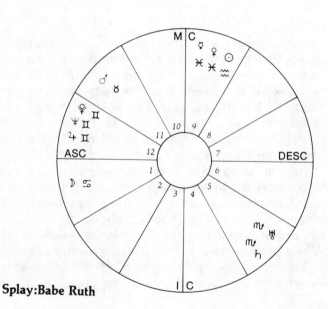

14

1. Thomas Jefferson

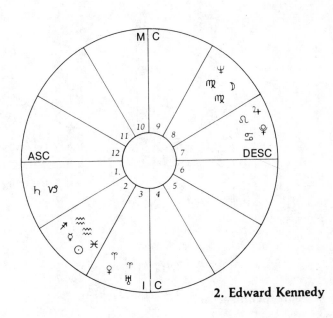

2. Edward Kennedy

3. George Wallace

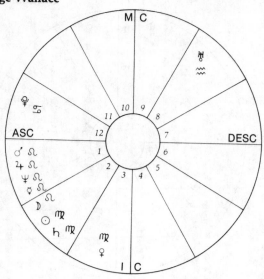

4. Eddie Rickenbacker

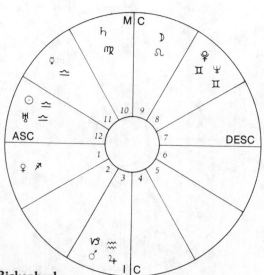

16

Homework Assignment

Temperament Patterns and Hemisphere Emphasis

A. Examine the four horoscopes on the preceding pages, and name the temperament pattern each horoscope has. (You may use your temperament pattern definitions).

1. Thomas Jefferson _____

2. Edward Kennedy _____

3. George Wallace _____

4. Eddie Rickenbacker _____

B. Place the number of the appropriate horoscope in the following blanks.

1. Which chart indicates a person with a wide variety of interests? _____

2. Which chart discloses a person of narrow interests who has a point of focus through which he must give back to the world?

_____

3. Which chart shows a dynamic, self-driving person who may have been a pioneer in some area? _____

4. Which chart reveals a need to balance? _____

C. Place the numbers (there may be none or more than one) of the appropriate horoscopes in the following blanks.

1. Which charts are those of individuals who tend more to have initiative and make their own opportunities? _____

2. Which charts are those of individuals whose opportunities generally come from others? _____

3. Which charts are those of individuals who usually adjust to the world? _____

4. Which charts are those of individuals who usually adjust the world to them? _____

2

HOUSES AND PLANETS

From this point on, the class period should be divided into three parts: I. Homework assignments; II. Introduction of new materials; III. Calculations.

Homework Assignments

By going around the class, with each student answering a question, class participation is assured.

When an answer is given that is not the one expected, it should be discussed. In astrology, because the components have more than one meaning, different answers to questions may be acceptable. The criterion is logic—if it fits it is correct. This, of course, only applies to matters subject to varying interpretations. With the homework assignment on hemisphere emphasis and temperament patterns, the hemisphere emphasis is objective (a count of planets in each hemisphere), so the student is either right or wrong. In the temperament patterns, more subjectivity is involved, so that if an answer is given which is not the one expected, the teacher could ask, "Why do you think it looks like that pattern? Does it describe the individual better than the other pattern? Or do both describe the individual?" By using this method of interpretation and discussing it in class, the students begin to combine the visual with logic.

An excellent example is Patricia Hearst, whose chart is

offered as the first calculation and interpretation. The arrangement of planets is "splashish" because they are in eight different houses, indicating an individual with many interests.

The arrangement is also "bucketish" with seven planets forming a bowl, while the Sun, Venus and Mercury form a handle. Here the distribution is 7-3 instead of 8-2 or 9-1, so it is not ideal; but Patricia Hearst—with the handle mainly in the seventh house—is one who experiences deeply and has an energy release or gives back to the world through "the other." Both patterns do describe her, and by coming to this realization in class, the students' understanding is deepened.

Introduction of new Materials.

The emphasis is on simplicity. Reference lists containing definitions for houses, planets, signs and aspects are distributed to the students. It is explained that the definitions are by no means exhaustive; in fact they can help trigger other definitions. Encourage reading introductory astrological texts in order to support the materials covered in class. The reference lists are offered primarily to help with the memorization. When interpretation is begun it is hoped that much of the material has been learned; but if it has not, referring to several lists is less disruptive to the flow of the thought process than having to leaf through a lengthy text.

The homework assignments are given to help with memorization. In the early assignments the answers coincide exactly with definitions on the reference sheets and with what is being introduced in class. In other words, the class material, reference lists and homework assignments provide three ways to help with memorization.

Houses are introduced first because they involve areas in the chart related to clearly understandable areas of life. There are no glyphs to memorize, only numbers 1 to 12 and definitions for each area. Explain that the houses derive their meaning from the natural zodiac, which begins with Aries, the first sign, and ends with Pisces, the last one.

After the houses have been defined individually, they are presented in oppositional pairs to show the connection between them and also to help the student realize that house 1 is in opposition to 7, 2 to 8, etc., which the student can relate to the picture of the chart when the visual chart is introduced.

1: the "I"; 7: the "thou." 2: our own resources; 8: other people's resources. 3: immediate environment (lower education, communications on a rudimentary level, short trips); 9: wider environment (higher education, dialogue on a philosophical level, long trips). 4: home, the more closely-linked parent; 10: the world, the more distantly-linked parent. 5: individual creativity; 11: group creativity. 6: physical health; 12: mental health. Students should be told that houses are numbered in a counterclockwise direction and that the beginning of each house is called the cusp of the house. It must also be explained that the planets and signs will have an important effect on the houses.

Planets are the function factors in the system. Each planet has a desirable and an undesirable manifestation, and both should be described. Definitions for the planets are on the second reference sheet, but, wherever possible, meanings can be reinforced by physical characteristics and mythological connections, or anything else the student might know that could aid in understanding and memorizing the symbolism of the planets. Some possibilities for each of the planets are:

Sun—shines, is visible, warms us, helps things grow so such definitions as will, outer self, ego can be understood.

Moon—has no light of its own, reflects light, and so corresponds to our responsive nature.

Mercury—was the messenger of the gods in mythology, therefore it is plausible that Mercury involves communications and those faculties of the mind, such as verbalization and logic, that enable us to communicate.

Venus—was the goddess of love and the arts, so *in* astrology she is still representative of them.

Mars—was the god of war, so the astrological definition

of aggression is appropriate. Mars is also called "the red planet," and we often associate red with anger, which is another possible manifestation of Mars.

Jupiter—is the largest planet in our solar system and also has a number of moons, therefore in astrology Jupiter is the planet of expansion.

Saturn—has rings around it, indicating containment, confinement, limitation and structure. The myth concerning Saturn's exile to an island which was in a state of chaos presents the structured, ordered side of Saturn, because on this island he formed an organized, prosperous society. Each year the citizens had a feast honoring Saturn for all he had done for them, which demonstrates the rewards of structure and hard work.

Uranus—was discovered in 1781, near the time of the American and French revolutions, and so represents liberation.

Neptune—was the god of the sea, evoking several meanings of the planet, such as nebulousness, illusion and lack of structure. This description is further supported by the lack of certainty as to exactly when Neptune was discovered and by whom.

Pluto—was the god of the underworld, representing in astrology what comes from the depths. Pluto was discovered in 1930 in the United States during the era of the gangster (another name for this element of our society is, of course, the "underworld").

Each planet rules a sign and will be correlated with it when the signs are discussed. There is a way, however, to memorize these correlations and to see the order in astrology quite easily. For this a circle is drawn and divided into twelfths, with a zodiacal sign in each section.

The lights (Moon and Sun) are placed outside the Cancer and the Leo section respectively—the Moon rules Cancer, the Sun, Leo. The next planet in terms of closeness to the Sun is Mercury, and Mercury rules the signs on either side of the lights: Gemini and Virgo. Venus is next and rules the signs Taurus and

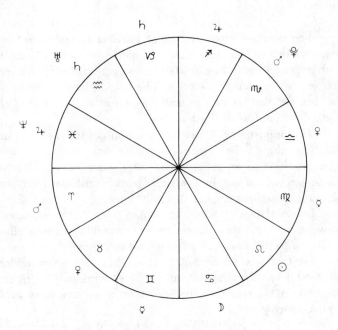

Planet-Sign Rulerships

Libra, on either side of the Mercury-ruled signs. Next is Mars, ruling Aries and Scorpio; then Jupiter, ruling Pisces and Sagittarius; and finally Saturn, ruling Capricorn and Aquarius. When the other three planets were discovered, they were assigned corulerships (Uranus, Aquarius; Neptune, Pisces; Pluto, Scorpio).

Calculations.

The example chart is that of Patricia Hearst. The emphemeris used is *The American Ephemeris*—samples of which are on pages 99 and 100. Calculation instructions are for a hand calculator with a single memory. The calculations are done in class, but detailed written instructions are given to the student for assistance in future chart casting.

The importance of having good sources for the birth information should be mentioned. The list of books and magazines that I consulted is on page 88. *Contemporary Sidereal Horoscopes*, which supplied Patricia Hearst's time uses birth certificates, the best source, for its birth times.

Before the calculations are begun, it must be explained that we are dealing with three different elements—sidereal time (pertaining to the stars), clock time and longitude.

We take sidereal time at 0 hours GMT on the Greenwich Birth Date from the first column in the ephemeris. This figure represents in sidereal time the point in space overhead at 0 hours, Greenwich Mean Time.

We are interested in the point overhead at the moment of birth, therefore we must know the Clock Time of birth and convert this to the Greenwich Mean Time of birth. Clock Time, however, is based on 24 hours as equivalent to 1 day, whereas sidereal time is based on a complete revolution of the earth in 1 day—which is 24 hours, 4+ minutes. Thus, clock time is converted to sidereal time by multiplying the Greenwich Mean Time of birth by 9.86 seconds and adding this number to the Greenwich Mean Time of Birth.

We must also make an adjustment for the exact longitude of birth, and therefore the longitude must also be converted to sidereal time. In order to do this, a student has to be told that 15 degrees of longitude = 1 hour of sidereal time; 1 degree of longitude = 4 minutes of sidereal time; 1 minute of longitude = 4 seconds of sidereal time. The result of the conversion is the Longitude Time Equivalent. The Longitude Time Equivalent for many localities can be found in *The American Ephemeris* (in the right-hand column of the section giving longitudes and latitudes of major cities), but by understanding the procedure the student can make this conversion if he has only the longitude of the birth locality. Now the actual chart casting can begin.

The instructions for casting Patricia Hearst's chart are given and calculation sheets are provided.

The teacher should not expect to do more than the house cusps on the first day of calculations. However, the calculations and the drawing of the chart must be finished by the time the material in Chapters 1-4 has been covered, so that the chart may be used when the work sheet is introduced in Chapter 5.

Homework should be assigned. Students ought to be told that besides the homework they should begin to draw and memorize the glyphs for the planets.

Basic Astrological Symbols and Concepts

Houses

1—The personality, physical appearance, and physical make-up; the house of the "I."

2—One's own possessions, finances, and other material resources; earning capacity, utilization of material objects, deep values.

3—Direct and immediate relations and communication, brothers and sisters, neighbors, short journeys.

4—Home, ancestry, origins, foundation, where one feels securely at home, house of the more closely-linked parent.

5—Creative self-expression; offspring, literal and figurative; love affairs, artistic creativity.

6—Physical health, service, routine, daily work.

7—Partnerships, including marriage; the public; open enemies.

8—Other peoples' possessions and finances, inheritance, death, sex, regeneration.

9—Philosophy, religion, law, world-view, long journeys, higher education.

10—Career, profession, relations with the outer world, house of the more distantly-linked parent.

11—Large groups and organizations, impersonal relationships, acquaintances, peers, hopes and wishes.

12—Concealment, mysticism, occultism, self-undoing, mental health, confinement (in prisons, hospitals, etc.), institutions.

Other Significant Points

ASC *Ascendant:* A point at which the meanings for the first house (see above) are intensified.

MC *Midheaven (medium coeli):* A point at which the meanings for the tenth house (see above) are intensified.

☊ *The Moon's Nodes:* Relationships and connections.

⊗ *The Part of Fortune:* A point signifying wholeness, integration, unity of self.

Planets

☉ *Sun:* Vitalization, the directly expressed self, exercise of ego-identity and will; the paternal function. Rules Leo.

☽ *Moon:* Response, emotion, intuition; the maternal function. Rules Cancer.

☿ *Mercury:* Verbal skills, communication, perception, logical thinking, cleverness, wit, which are functions of the "lower mind." Rules Gemini and Virgo.

♀ *Venus:* Love, affection, pleasure, artistry, harmonization; female sexuality. Rules Taurus and Libra.

♂ *Mars:* Initiative, aggressive action, courage, violence, passion; male sexuality. Rules Aries, co-rules Scorpio (with Pluto).

♃ *Jupiter:* Wide-ranging and complex thinking, wisdom, which are functions of the "higher mind;" joy, optimism, success, excess; expansion. Rules Sagittarius, co-rules Pisces (with Neptune).

♄ *Saturn:* Contraction, containment, crystallization, responsibility, structure, discipline, channeling, limitation, restriction,frustration, gloom, pessimism; punishment. Rules Capricorn and co-rules Aquarius (with Uranus).

♅ *Uranus:* Deviation, liberation, sudden or revolutionary change; technique and technology. Co-rules Aquarius (with Saturn).

♆ *Neptune:* Refined sensitivity, spirituality, dissolution, confusion, illusion, intoxication; ethereal and spiritual artistry. Co-rules Pisces (with Jupiter).

♇ *Pluto:* Total transformation through elimination and renewal, violence, subterranean (subconscious) eruption, unrelenting power; deep probing and analysis. Co-rules Scorpio (with Mars).

Signs

♈ *Aries:* Self-assertiveness, aggressiveness, zeal, naivete; the "eager-beaver" and "me-first" sign. Ruled by Mars.

♉ *Taurus:* Practicality, persistence, domination by habit, stubbornness, possessiveness; the "artsy-craftsy" sign. Ruled by Venus.

♊ *Gemini:* Adaptability, flexibility, fluctuation, gregariousness, articulateness, two-sidedness; the sociability sign. Ruled by Mercury.

♋ *Cancer:* Motherliness, protectiveness, self-protectiveness, sensitivity, moodiness, deep emotionality, intuitiveness; the "homebody" sign. Ruled by the Moon.

♌ *Leo:* Warm-heartedness, generosity, magnanimity, pomposity, dominating or domineering tendencies; the sign of the king or the actor. Ruled by the Sun.

♍ *Virgo:* Painstaking industriousness, devotedness to service, analytical and critical tendencies, interest in health and hygiene, hypochondria, detail-orientation; "fussbudget" of the Zodiac. Ruled by Mercury.

♎ *Libra:* Harmony, need for partnerships and marriage, artistic and aesthetic values, diplomacy and tact, indolence, indecisiveness; the balancing sign. Ruled by Venus.

♏ *Scorpio:* Emotional intensity, hard-driving and persistent aggressiveness, loyalty, pessimism; preoccupation with sex, death and regeneration; secretiveness; the sign of probing and penetrating. Co-ruled by Mars and Pluto.

♐ *Sagittarius:* Enthusiasm; urge to travel far and wide, both mentally and physically; interest in fun, athletics, the out-of-doors and animals; the sign of the "jovial philosopher." Ruled by Jupiter.

♑ *Capricorn:* Ambition, patience; tendencies to be conventional, conservative and traditional; status-orientation, discipline, strong sense of duty; the unrelenting climber of the Zodiac. Ruled by Saturn.

♒ *Aquarius:* Humanitarian idealism, impersonal detachment, urge to liberate or be liberated, nonconformity, egalitarianism; the liberal or revolutionary of the Zodiac. Co-ruled by Saturn and Uranus.

♓ *Pisces:* Compassion, empathy, self-sacrifice, intuitiveness, mysticism, spiritualism, nebulousness, vulnerability to delusion and/or victimization; the sign of suffering and/or salvation. Co-ruled by Jupiter and Neptune.

Aspects

☌ *Conjunction* (0°): Strong but mixed in quality, depending on the planets involved.

☍ *Opposition* (180°): Hard; a need to balance or may be separative; an aspect of relationship.

△ *Trine* (120°): Soft; what flows easily.

□ *Square* (90°): Hard; obstacles to be overcome; may be building blocks or stumbling blocks.

✳ *Sextile* (60°): Soft; like the trine but less powerful; an aspect of help from others.

⊻ *Semi-sextile* (30°): Mixed and mild.

⚻ *Quincunx* (150°): Mixed and moderately strong; an aspect combining quite different or contradictory things; therefore, often quite difficult to evaluate.

Q *Quintile* (72°): Soft, subtle; involves creativity.

± *Bi-quintile* (144°): Same as quintile.

∠ *Semi-square* (45°): Same as square but less powerful.

⚼ *Sesqui-quadrate* (135°): Same as semi-square.

Major Configurations

T-Square: Two planets in opposition, and a third planet square to both—usually in the same mode (cardinal, fixed, mutable).

Grand Cross: Two planets in opposition and square two other planets in opposition—usually in the same mode.

Grand Trine: Three planets in trine to each other—usually in the same element (fire, earth, air, water).

Yod (or Finger of God): Two planets sextile each other, and both quincunx a third.

Cradle: Four planets in a series of sextiles.

Cradle with a Hood: Five planets in a series of sextiles.

Homework Assignment

Houses and Planets

A.   The numbers in the left-hand column are the numbers of the houses. The words in columns two and three are definitions for the houses. Place the letters of the definitions next to the appropriate house number. There will be two answers for each.

1. _____	a. open enemies	m. other people's money
2. _____	b. physical health	n. the home
3. _____	c. distant travel	o. the personality
4. _____	d. marriage partners	p. career
5. _____	e. organizations such as clubs	q. values
6. _____	f. short journeys	r. creative self-expression
7. _____	g. relations with the outer world	s. one's own earning capacity
8. _____	h. philosophy	t. peer groups
9. _____	i. physical appearance	u. communications
10. _____	j. one's origins	v. children
11. _____	k. daily work	w. death
12. _____	l. mental health	x. institutions

B.   In the first column are the planets. In columns two and three are two definitions for each planet. Place the letters of the appropriate definitions next to the appropriate planet.

☉ Sun _____	a. originality	k. elimination
☾ Moon _____	b. spiritualism	l. frustration
☿ Mercury _____	c. love	m. aggressiveness
♀ Venus _____	d. expansion	n. artistry
♂ Mars _____	e. responsibility	o. lower mind
♃ Jupiter _____	f. illusion	p. power

♄ Saturn _____ g. revolutionary activity q. responsiveness
♅ Uranus _____ h. the will   r. initiative
♆ Neptune _____ i. optimism   s. cleverness
♇ Pluto _____ j. the maternal function t. exercise of ego identity

C. Multiple choice. For one possible manifestation of the planet in the house, circle the appropriate answer.

1. Initiative in career
a. ♀ in 5th house   b. ♂ in 10th house   c. ♄ in 8th house

2. Wants power over partner
a. ☉ in 3rd house   b. ☿ in 9th house   c. ♀ in 7th house

3. Gets an advanced degree in philosophy
a. ♃ in 9th house   b. ♂ in 4th house   c. ☾ in 12th house

4. Responsibility in the home
a. ♄ in 4th house   b. ♆ in 6th house   c. ♅ in 2nd house

5. Moodiness
a. ☿ in 11th house   b. ☾ in 1st house   c. ♃ in 10th house

6. Communicates in a confused way
a. ♅ in 2nd house   b. ♄ in 7th house   c. ♆ in 3rd house

7. Originality with peer groups
a. ☉ in 12th house   b. ♅ in 11th house   c. ♀ in 2nd house

8. Ego involvement with children
a. ♆ in 9th house   b. ☿ in 6th house   c. ☉ in 5th house

9. Earning one's own living through cleverness
a. ☿ in 2nd house   b. ☉ in 11th house   c. ♅ in 4th house

10. Artistry as part of daily work
a. ♂ in 8th house   b. ♀ in 6th house   c. ♄ in 12th house

3

SIGNS

Homework assignments.

The purpose of the assignment given after you have covered the houses and planets is to familiarize the students with meanings for the houses and planets, (sections A and B), to help them begin to recognize the glyphs (sections B and C) and to start the integration process (section C). The answers in section C combine the definitions in A and B.

Introduction of new materials.

The twelve signs of the Zodiac represent characteristics, and it is with the signs that one begins to grasp the tightly integrated nature of the system. All twelve signs are part of everyone's life, since they are all present in everyone's horoscope; but how and where these characteristics are expressed depends on which planets are in each sign and which signs are in each house.

In Chapter 2 we began to see the order in astrology by examining the rulerships of the signs. Before the individual signs are discussed, more information can be added to further illustrate the orderliness of proper astrological practice, and also to assist in the understanding of the signs.

Each sign, besides having a ruler, also represents an *element*. There are four elements: fire, signifying enthusiasm, zeal

Sign	Glyph	Symbol	House Connection	Element	Mode	Polarity	Ruler	Parts of the Body	Key words
Aries	♈	Ram	1	Fire	Cardinal	+	♂	Head and Face	
Taurus	♉	Bull	2	Earth	Fixed	−	♀	Neck and Throat	
Gemini	♊	Twins	3	Air	Mutable	+	☿	Hands, Arms Lungs	
Cancer	♋	Crab	4	Water	Cardinal	−	☾	Stomach, Breast	
Leo	♌	Lion	5	Fire	Fixed	+	☉	Heart, Upper Spine	
Virgo	♍	Virgin	6	Earth	Mutable	−	☿	Intestines	
Libra	♎	Scales	7	Air	Cardinal	+	♀	Kidneys, Lower Spine	
Scorpio	♏	Scorpion	8	Water	Fixed	−	♂ ♇	Sex Organs, Bladder, Anus	
Sagittarius	♐	Archer	9	Fire	Mutable	+	♃	Thighs, Liver	
Capricorn	♑	Mountain Goat	10	Earth	Cardinal	−	♄	Knees	
Aquarius	♒	Water Bearer	11	Air	Fixed	+	♄ ♅	Calves and Ankles	
Pisces	♓	Fish	12	Water	Mutable	−	♃ ♆	Feet	

and warmth; earth (practicality and materialism); air (mental activity and abstraction); and water (emotions and intuition). Using the chart on page 23 place an element in each sign. Start with Aries, fire; Taurus, earth; Gemini, air; Cancer, water; etc. and continue around the Zodiac until each sign contains an element. The four groups of three signs representing the same element are called the triplicities.

Each sign also has a *mode*. There are three modes: cardinal, signifying initiative and interest in direct involvement in situations; fixed, (persistence and goal orientation); mutable (fluctuation, adaptability and interest in people). Again beginning with Aries, we go around the zodiac with the modes. Aries is cardinal; Taurus, fixed; Gemini, mutable; etc. The three groups of four signs having the same mode are called the quadruplicities. Each sign then has an element and a mode, but no combination is repeated.

Polarity is also ascribed to each sign. All of the odd-numbered signs (Aries, Gemini, etc.) are positive, and the even-numbered signs (Taurus, Cancer, etc.) are negative. These attributions too may be placed in the chart within each sign (written as + for positive, − for negative). There are several definitions given to polarity, but recently a study done in England showed a high correlation between polarity and psychological tests for extroversion-introversion.* The positive Sun signs were extroverted, the negative Sun signs, introverted. However, the total number of planets in positive and negative signs seems more significant for interpretation than the polarity of a single planet.

All of the parts studied so far (houses, planets, elements, modes and polarity) can now be combined in the discussion of signs. Because of the breadth of the material, it should take two weeks to cover the signs, with the first six signs discussed the first week and the last six signs the second week.

---

*"British Scientist Proves Basic Astrology Theory," *Phenomena*, 1.1, (April 1, 1977) pp. 1-2.

Have the students draw ten columns with the headings given on the chart on page 36. The teacher should do the same on the board and discuss each box as it is filled in. When the first nine boxes are completed, the class will decide on appropriate key words under the direction of the teacher.

As an example, Aries. Under *Glyph*, ♈ should be drawn. The glyph depicts ram's horns, and the *Symbol* is the ram. What does the ram do? It puts down its head and butts forward. Sometimes it butts into a wall without thinking about the consequences. The *House Connection* is 1—the first house is the me-first house; Aries, the me-first sign. (It is important to memorize the numbers with the signs—Aries, 1; Taurus, 2; etc.—because it will be helpful later for numerous reasons.) The *Element* is fire, representing enthusiasm, warmth, zeal and an involvement in situations. The *Mode* is cardinal (initiating). The *Polarity* is + (extroverted). The *Ruler* is Mars, again showing initiative and action. The *Parts of the Body* are the head and face. This is hardly the sign of a recluse or procrastinator. What are the possible *Key Words?* Aggressiveness and "outgoingness" are two.

When the signs of the Zodiac are completed, the miscellanea should be covered.

Retrograde planets: the energy of the planet becomes internal or is slow in developing.

Part of Fortune: this point is where the Moon would be if the Sun were on the Ascendant. Since the Part of Fortune combines the Sun, Moon and Ascendant (forming a kind of core of the person), it represents a point of wholeness, and the house in which it is posited is important for the personality.

Nodes of the Moon: relations with the world, and the houses and signs in which the Nodes are posited indicate ways the individual can relate to others. The South Node of the Moon is always opposite the North Node.

Calculations.

Calculation of planetary positions should be begun (refer to the calculation form beginning on page 90). It will probably take at least two lessons to complete the calculations.

Assign homework after the first six signs are discussed, and after the last six signs are discussed.

Homework Assignment

First Six Signs of the Zodiac

A.   All other things being equal, which sign would make the better:

1. Secretary: Virgo ♍ , or Leo ♌
2. Playboy: Gemini ♊ , or Cancer ♋
3. Actor or Actress: Virgo ♍ , or Leo ♌
4. Governess: Aries ♈ , or Cancer ♋
5. Craftsman: Taurus ♉ , or Aries ♈
6. Salesman: Virgo ♍ , or Aries ♈

B.   Emphasis of a sign (which may come from planets, Ascendant or MC being placed in the sign) will indicate certain characteristics. In which signs would the following characteristics most likely be manifested?

1. Stubbornness: Aries ♈ , or Taurus ♉
2. Sociability: Gemini ♊ , or Virgo ♍
3. Personal magnetism: Leo ♌ , or Cancer ♋
4. Meticulousness: Leo ♌ , or Virgo ♍
5. Initiative: Taurus ♉ , or Aries ♈
6. Motherliness: Gemini ♊ , or Cancer ♋

C.   Venus (♀) represents love. Indications of love can be found in various ways in different areas of the chart; but considering just Venus (♀) in the first six signs, which word would best describe how the individual would love?

1. Would ♀ in ♈ be aggressive or shy?
2. Would ♀ in ♉ be fickle or loyal?
3. Would ♀ in ♊ be fickle or loyal?
4. Would ♀ in ♋ be selfish or protective?
5. Would ♀ in ♌ be warm or dispassionate?
6. Would ♀ in ♍ be practical or impractical?

Homework Assignment

Last Six Signs of the Zodiac

A.   All other things being equal, which sign would make the better:

1. Occultist: Capricorn ♑ , or Pisces ♓
2. Revolutionary: Aquarius ♒ , or Pisces ♓
3. Surgeon: Scorpio ♏ , or Aquarius ♒
4. Artist: Sagittarius ♐ , or Libra ♎
5. President of a company: Capricorn ♑ , or Libra ♎
6. World traveler: Scorpio ♏ , or Sagittarius ♐

B.   Emphasis of a sign (which may come from planets, Ascendant or MC being placed in the sign) will indicate certain characteristics. In which signs would the following characteristics most likely be manifested?

1. Conservatism: Capricorn ♑ , or Aquarius ♒
2. Pessimism: Sagittarius ♐ , or Scorpio ♏
3. Empathy: Capricorn ♑ , or Pisces ♓
4. Joviality: Sagittarius ♐ , or Scorpio ♏
5. Balance: Libra ♎ , or Pisces ♓
6. Cause-orientation: Aquarius ♒ , or Libra ♎

C. Venus (♀) represents love. Indications of love can be found in various ways in different areas of the chart; but considering just Venus (♀) in the last six signs, which word would best describe how the individual would love?

1. Would ♀ in ♎ be erratic or balanced?
2. Would ♀ in ♏ be emotional or cool?
3. Would ♀ in ♐ be fickle or loyal?
4. Would ♀ in ♑ be demonstrative or reserved?
5. Would ♀ in ♒ be possessive or impersonal?
6. Would ♀ in ♓ be selfish or self-sacrificing?

Homework Assignment

The Signs of the Zodiac

A. Write the names of the signs of the Zodiac and draw the glyphs in numerical order (e.g., 1. Aries ♈ , etc.). Then circle the characteristic adjective which is appropriate for that sign.

1. _____ is outgoing, passive.
2. _____ is stubborn, flexible.
3. _____ is unfriendly, sociable.
4. _____ is home-loving, career-oriented.
5. _____ is cold, warm.
6. _____ is sloppy, meticulous.
7. _____ is balanced, flighty.
8. _____ is shallow, intense.
9. _____ is morose, jovial.
10. _____ is conservative, radical.
11. _____ is passionate, interested in humanitarian causes.
12. _____ is sensitive, insensitive.

B. Triplicities:

   1. Name the three fire signs._____
   2. Name the three earth signs._____
   3. Name the three air signs._____
   4. Name the three water signs._____

C. Quadruplicities:

   1. Name the four cardinal signs._____
   2. Name the four fixed signs._____
   3. Name the four mutable signs._____

4

ASPECTS AND MAJOR CONFIGURATIONS

Homework Assignments

The homework assignment on the signs should be covered, and at the end of the class the assignment on major configurations distributed.

Introduction of new materials

The various aspects would be discussed first and then combinations of aspects forming major configurations could be explained.

Aspects. The quality of the aspects (hard, soft, mixed) should be given, as well as a short, clear definition of each. (Definitions are on p. 29.)

The orbs that I use are 8° for major aspects (conjunction, opposition, trine, square and sextile) and 2° for minor aspects. In other words, the trine would be from 112° to 128°, and the semi-sextile from 28° to 32°. I sometimes extend these orbs, for instance, when one planet that is slightly out of orb of an aspect to a second planet is conjunct a third planet that is within orb of that aspect. Another exception is when one planet in a major configuration (such as a T-Square) aspects two other planets which are slightly out of orb.

Major Configurations. The major configurations combine three or more planets and/or points. These configurations indicate more intricate patterns than do individual aspects, since more of the chart is included, and aspects of differing qualities are combined. Remember to examine both the possible desirable and undesirable manifestations.

T-Square. The T-Square connects at least three planets or points, of which two are in opposition and the third is in square to both. This configuration combines the definition of the square (obstacles to be overcome or conflicts to be resolved) with the opposition (a need to balance). The quality is hard, but when used positively the T-Square can be a source of energy and strength. Since the planets or points are in square relationship, they are usually in the same mode (cardinal, fixed or mutable), and the mode further explains how the patterns will be manifested. An excellent description of the modes is given in *Finding the Person in the Horoscope* by Zipporah Dobyns, pp. 18-19. Dr. Dobyns suggests you "imagine two cars reaching an intersection simultaneously, at a ninety degree angle to each other." With the T-Square there will be three "cars."

Cardinal: "The cardinal cars arrive, crash, one flips on its back, and the other charges off at a new angle." *Fixed:* "The fixed cars approach the intersection...get their noses together, and hold, in a state of impasse with neither giving an inch...Fixed signs represent enduring self-will." *Mutable:* "The mutable cars never get close enough to each other to touch. One car veers in one direction and the other goes around it and they circle and try again in a kind of dance. Mutables live in the head, with a flexibility and versatility that promotes constant change."

Grand Cross. The Grand Cross has the same quality as the T-Square and also is usually in a single mode. This configuration is a little more intricate in that it adds another planet or point and the fourth sign of a mode. It has two oppositions which are square to each other.

Grand Trine. The Grand Trine involves three or more planets or points which are approximately 120° from each other, forming three trines. The quality is soft. Positively, it indicates what flows easily in the chart—negatively, what can flow too easily and "run away with you." Since the planets are 120° apart, they are usually in the same element (fire, earth, air, water). The element adds further understanding of how the pattern will be manifested.

Fire: A fire Grand Trine positively may signify the flow of enthusiasm, zeal, warmth; negatively, one can undertake too much. *Earth:* An earth Grand Trine positively may indicate one who is practical and goal-oriented—negatively, one who is dull or ruthless. *Air:* An air Grand Trine positively may connote one who has mental facility and ability to deal with ideas or abstractions—negatively, one who rationalizes or is impractical. *Water:* A water Grand Trine positively may indicate one who is compassionate, sympathetic and highly intuitive—negatively, one who is ruled by sheer emotions and fantasy.

Yod. In a Yod, two planets are in sextile to each other, and both quincunx a third planet. This is a mixed configuration and usually suggests a radical change at some time in the life in terms of these planets (particularly the planet that is quincunxed) or the houses that these planets occupy or rule. Since both the sextile and the quincunx often involve other persons, the change may be precipitated by someone else.

Cradle. The Cradle connects four or more planets or points by sextile, with the first and last planet forming an opposition. This configuration is basically soft (a series of sextiles) with some balance needed (the opposition). It indicates help from outside—thus the situation of an individual who at some point is standing in the right place at the right time.

Cradle with a Hood. A Cradle with a Hood connects five or more planets or points by sextile, and in this case there are two oppositions. It has the same meaning as the Cradle and retains its essential softness, but because there are more aspects and another planet, it is a little more intricate than the Cradle.

Chart Number 1

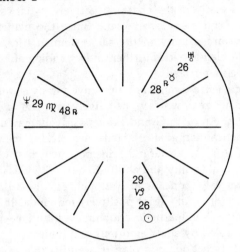

Calculations.

Calculations should be completed and the chart drawn by the time the material in this chapter is covered, so that the chart may be used with the work sheet which will be introduced next.

Homework Assignment

Major Configurations

A.   Each of the charts contains a major configuration. Place the correct chart number next to each configuration listed below.

1. A Grand Trine in
   Water   _____

2. A Yod   _____

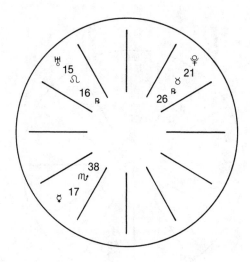

3. A Grand Trine in
   Earth   _____

4. A fixed T-Square   _____

5. A Cradle   _____

6. A mutable T-Square _____

B. Below are possible manifestations of each major configuration. Place the correct chart number next to each description.

    1. Help will come from outside. This individual will be
      standing in the right place, at the right time, at some
      point in his or her life._____

    2. There will be a definite change at some point in this in-
      dividual's life._____

Chart Number 3

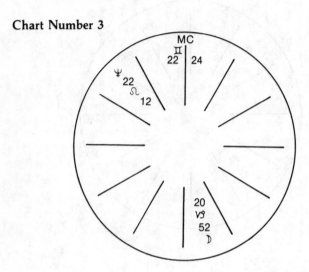

3. This person may have the stick-to-it-iveness to overcome obstacles in life. He or she could also be stubborn._____

4. This person will be practical and may receive "gains"during his or her lifetime._____

5. This individual will be adaptable or changeable. When obstacles or problems appear, there might be a floundering from one decision to another._____

6. The positive expression is empathy and sympathy; the negative is that emotions may "run away" with this individual._____

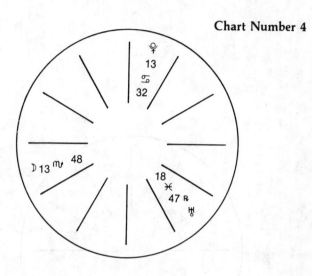

Chart Number 4

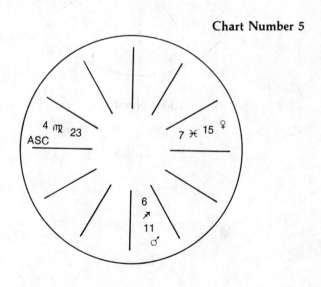

Chart Number 5

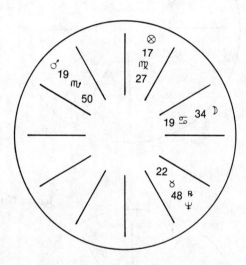

Chart Number 6

5

WORKSHEET

Homework assignments.

Review the homework assignment for the major configurations in class. At the end of the class, after the work sheet on Patricia Hearst is completed, the next homework assignment should be given. The questions will reinforce the material on the worksheet.

It is possible that all the material on the worksheet will not be covered in a single class period. In this case intermediate homework assignments on Patricial Hearst's chart can be given, such as: write a paragraph combining the characteristics of her Sun, Moon and Ascendant signs; how does the sign emphasis by sign and by house add to what the Sun, Moon and Ascendant signs tell us of the personality; what do hemisphere emphasis and temperament pattern contribute to the total picture of the personality, etc. These assignments may be somewhat repetitive, but this repetition will help to reinforce the method, and the assignment will provide a review as well as further reinforcement.

Introduction of new materials.

Because a horoscope contains all of the factors introduced in Chapters 1-4, a student examining a chart for the first time is usually overwhelmed. With the use of a worksheet, the many

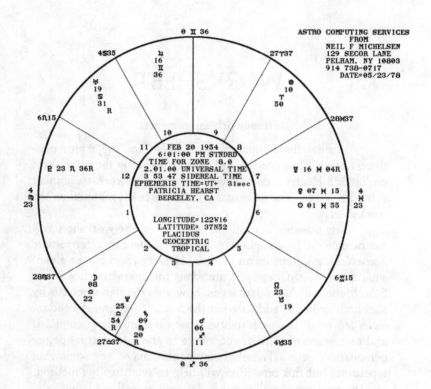

0 ♊ 36

4♋35

♃
16
♊
36

27♈37

♅
19
♋
31
R

⊗
10
♈
50

6♌15

28♓37

10   9

11   FEB 20 1954   8
6:01:00 PM STNDRD
TIME FOR ZONE 8.0
2.01.00 UNIVERSAL TIME
3 53 47 SIDEREAL TIME
EPHEMERIS TIME=UT+ 31sec
PATRICIA HEARST
BERKELEY, CA

12   7

♇ 23 ♌ 36R

☿ 16 ♓ 04R

♀ 07 ♓ 15

☉ 01 ♓ 55

4
♏
23

4
♓
23

LONGITUDE=122W16
LATITUDE= 37N52
PLACIDUS
GEOCENTRIC
TROPICAL

1   6

2   5

3   4

28♍37

☽
08
♎
22

♆
25
♎
54
R

♄
09
♏
20
R

♂
06
♐
11

6♏15

♊
23
♐
19

27♎37

4♐35

0 ♐ 36

ASTRO COMPUTING SERVICES
FROM
NEIL F MICHELSEN
129 SECOR LANE
PELHAM, NY 10803
914 738-0717
DATE=05/23/78

Worksheet

Name **Patricia Hearst**

Sun ♓ ___ Moon ♎ ___ Ascendant ♍ ___ Stellium ♓ ___

Ascendant Ruler ☿ House **7** MC Ruler ☿ House **7**

Elements, by Sign: by House: Hemisphere Emphasis:

Fire ♀ ♂ ___   ___   East **6**

Earth **Asc** ___   ☽ ♀ ☉ ♃   West **4**

Air ♃ ☽ ♆ MC ___   ♄ ♀ ☿ ♅   South **5**

Water ♅ ♄ ☊ ♀ ☿   ♂ ♇   North **5**

Modes: Polarity:

Cardinal ♅ ☽ ♆ ___   ♂ ♀ ☿ ♃   Positive **5**

Fixed ♇ ♄ ___   ☽ ♆ ♅   Negative **5**

Mutable ♃ ☉ ☊ ♀ ☿ MC A ___ ♄ ☊ ♇   Temperament Pattern:

Sign Emphasis: ♓ ♑ ♎   **Splashish-bucketish**

Domal Planets ___   Mutual Reception ♀/♆ ☿/♃

Most Elevated Planet **♃**   Planet Rising ♀

Planet Rising before ☉ **♂**   Planet Last
Conjuncted by ☽ ♇

Major Configurations, etc.:

Mutable Grand Cross

Cardinal T-Square

Grand Trine in Water

parts are put into order, and the interpretation becomes simpler. The worksheet should include both general information for the initial overall view of the chart and specific information for more in-depth analysis. The worksheet material can be interpreted step-by-step or when the sheet is completed. It is best for beginning students to interpret each blank as it is filled, successively adding to the preceding information and modifying or supporting it. By using Patricia Hearst's chart and the worksheet, a specific example of the procedure can be given.

Sun. Patricia Hearst's Sun is in Pisces. Thus she is emotional, compassionate, sensitive, possibly self-sacrificing, mutable or adaptable.

Moon. The Moon is in Libra, indicating an emotional interest (the Moon) in the other, and a need for harmony and balance. Libra is an air sign, and therefore the mental is important. Both the Sun and Moon signs show an emphasis on relationships, and possibly helping others or being dependent upon them.

Ascendant. The Ascendant in Virgo, which is a service-oriented sign, adds a new idea related to needing and perhaps helping others. Virgo is an earth sign and can lend some practicality to the Pisces water and the Libra air; but it is mutable, thus the practicality may fluctuate. There is also the possibility that Virgo will become so involved in details that it will lose sight of the goal. The combination of Virgo, Pisces and Libra indicates that the needs and desires of others will be so strongly emphasized one's personal goals may be neglected.

Stellium. A stellium is three or more planets in the same sign or house. Planets in a sign signify that the expression of the energies of the planets is accompanied by the characteristics of the sign. Planets in a house denote specific functions connected with that house, and also more subtle characteristics of the natural sign connected with the house (e.g., a first-house stellium will indicate definite attributes of the personality and also some Aries traits).

Patricia Hearst has a stellium in Pisces (Sun in the sixth

house, and Venus and Mercury in the seventh), which makes the characteristics of her Sun sign even stronger. The Sun implies ego involvement or vital energy; Venus, love; and Mercury, communication. She therefore has a Pisces ego, and loves and communicates in a Piscean way.

Ascendant Ruler (also called the ruler of the chart) is Mercury, showing the importance of communications and the lower mind in the total personality.

House placement of the Ascendant Ruler reveals a specific connection between the general personality and the house involved. In Patricia Hearst's chart the ruler, Mercury, is in the seventh house indicating a self-identification with, or surrender to, the "other" or partner. The Libran message is repeated, and the need with the Virgo and Pisces for other people is supported.

MC Ruler. The Midheaven ruler, which is also Mercury, is important in the impression she makes on the world at large. Mercury (the MC ruler) may be correlated with the career later when it is discussed.

House placement of the MC ruler. Since the ruler is in the seventh house, there is also an intimate connection between the "other" or the partner and Patricia Hearst's role in the world.

Elements and Modes by Sign. In these blanks we place the planets, MC and Ascendant in their elements (fire, earth, air or water) and modes (cardinal, fixed or mutable) and note the element and the mode with the highest total. This procedure is another way to examine sign emphasis. Patricia Hearst has Pluto and Mars in fire signs; Ascendant in earth; Jupiter, Moon, Neptune and MC in air; and Uranus, Saturn, Sun, Venus and Mercury in water. The highest count by element is in water. In cardinal signs she has Uranus, Moon and Neptune; in fixed, Pluto and Saturn; and in mutable, Jupiter, Mars, Sun, Venus, Mercury, MC and Ascendant. The highest count by mode is in mutable. The mutable water sign is Pisces, providing even more evidence of the strength of the characteristics of this sign in Patricia Hearst's chart. Pisces is written in the blank marked *Sign Emphasis* under *by Sign*.

Elements and Modes by House. Since houses have a strong connection with the signs, we can obtain more information by counting the planets according to the elements and modes *of the houses* in which they are posited. Because the Ascendant and Midheaven are dividing lines for the houses, they cannot be used. The fire houses are 1, 5 and 9; the earth houses are 2, 6 and 10; the air houses, 3, 7 and 11; and the water houses are 4, 8 and 12. One, 4, 7 and 10 are the cardinal or angular houses; 2, 5, 8 and 11, the fixed or succedent houses; and 3, 6, 9 and 12 are the mutable or cadent houses. Patricia Hearst has no planets in the fire houses; Moon, Neptune, Sun and Jupiter in earth houses; Saturn, Venus, Mercury and Uranus in air houses; and Mars and Pluto in water houses. Mars, Venus, Mercury and Jupiter are in cardinal houses; Moon, Neptune and Uranus are in fixed houses; and Saturn, Sun and Pluto are in mutable houses. The highest count by element is in earth and air; and by mode, cardinal is a little stronger than fixed or mutable. The emphasis, therefore, is cardinal earth (Capricorn) and cardinal air (Libra), which are written in the blank marked *Sign Emphasis* under *by House.* The Libra emphasis supports characteristics we have already discussed, but Capricorn adds something new—the possibility of conservatism, ambition, persistence, etc. These characteristics might help to balance the mutability, emotionality and dependence on others, but a lot of effort would probably have to be exerted since Pisces and Libra—with totally different qualities—are very strong.

Hemisphere Emphasis. There are six eastern planets and four western planets, indicating that Patricia Hearst can initiate a little more than respond. However, the possibility of her initiative being latent or more subtle than direct is strong because of the Pisces, Libra and Virgo emphasis. For instance, she might have to weigh what others wanted or how others would feel before she acted. There are five northern planets and five southern planets, showing that she can both adjust the world to her and adjust herself to the world.

Polarity. With five positive planets and five negative planets there is a balance between extroversion and introversion.

Temperament Pattern. Her temperament pattern is not clear-cut. We can eliminate the Bundle (planets are not concentrated within a trine); Seesaw (not enough planets in opposition); Locomotive (no empty trine); Bowl (planets are not concentrated in one-half of the chart); Splay (not enough concentration since eight houses are occupied.) We are left with the Splash and the Bucket. When eight houses are occupied the chart is a Splash. This chart, however, is also "Bucketish," although not the ideal Bucket. Seven planets (instead of eight or nine) are evenly spaced within one-half of the chart and three planets (instead of one or two) are widely conjunct (Sun, Venus, Mercury) in the other half. We can combine the meanings of these two patterns and add them to the information we already have. Patricia Hearst has a number of interests (Splashish) but will probably not be the universal woman, since her mutability does not provide the "stick-to-it-iveness" needed to concentrate deeply in many areas. She also develops through experience and gives back to the world through Sun, Venus and Mercury in Pisces in the sixth and seventh houses (Bucketish). This interpretation is strongly supported by what we have already discovered (the importance of others, particularly a partner—Pisces, Libra; the possibility of serving— Virgo).

Domal Planets (planets in their own signs). A planet in its own sign indicates that the planet is strong in the chart but does not specify whether it is good or bad. Patricia Hearst has no domal planets.

Mutual Reception. She has two mutual receptions—Venus-Neptune, and Mercury-Jupiter. Planets in mutual reception work together in some way. The Venus-Neptune might indicate artistic ability, spiritual love or deception in love. The Mercury-Jupiter might show that the lower and higher minds blend, that communications are widely directed, or that there might be exaggeration in communicating. Since

Mercury and Jupiter are square each other, as well as being in mutual reception, there will probably have to be a working out of problems or obstacles concerning the lower and higher minds or communications.

Most Elevated Planet. If this planet is within 5° of the MC, the planet will have a strong effect on the impression one makes. The farther it is from the MC, the less consistent the impression becomes in terms of the planet. Jupiter is Patricia Hearst's most elevated planet, but it is 16° from the MC, so the possible "jovial" impression that Jupiter could provide might be intermittent.

Planet Rising. Pluto is rising. Although it is 10° from the Ascendant, and therefore not as strong as it would be if it were closer, it still alters the Virgo somewhat, as evidenced by the penetrating eyes. Pluto also might indicate a person who is sometimes deeply analytical or one who might experience a personality transformation.

Planet Rising before the Sun. The planet rising before the Sun is Mars, suggesting that she has some initiative, but with all her mutability (including Mars being in Sagittarius) and her dependence on others, she would not be extremely aggressive. Though she allegedly fired the gun at the sporting goods robbery, she probably would not have done so if her friends, the Harrises, had not been in trouble.

Planet Last Conjuncted by the Moon. The Moon is associated with change, and the planet last conjuncted by the Moon before birth shows how one adjusts to change. For Patricia Hearst, this planet is Pluto in Leo. She either analyzes change deeply (Pluto) or can change her self-expression (Leo) completely.

By now you should have a general idea of Patricia Hearst, which can be summarized with a few key words or phrases such as: emotionality, interest in mental and communicative activities; close involvement with others and, very likely, dependence upon them; flexibility or fluctuation and adaptability; capability of total change.

Major Configurations: As we examine the major configurations in terms of the aspects and planets, we can determine some of the major patterns of her life and add to the total picture. She has a mutable Grand Cross involving the MC (her public image or the impression she makes), the Ascendant (her personality), her initiating ability (Mars), her vital energy or ego (Sun) and love or pleasure (Venus). The planets and points are interconnected and, therefore, describe an intricate pattern. The mutable mode shows a fluctuation; the squares indicate conflicts or obstacles that have to be faced; and the oppositions, a need to balance. We can look at the configuration in terms of any of the planets or points and form a coherent picture. For instance, examining her initiating ability (Mars), we know that there is a lack of consistency in her initiative because Mars is in the mutable sign of Sagittarius. She would also have to work on obstacles or conflicts involving her personality (Ascendant), ego (Sun) and love (Venus) before she could initiate, because those planets and point square the Mars. The opposition between Mars and the MC would also show a need to balance her public image with her ability to initiate. We can further determine that the signs involved in the squares are not forceful signs (Virgo and Pisces), so she would not have the push nor the confidence to act aggressively. How could she be helped to initiate? We would look to the soft Mars aspects for this help. We find that the only soft aspect is Moon sextile Mars, so she could probably initiate best and most easily in response to others.

Patricia Hearst also has a cardinal T-Square consisting of Uranus conjunct the South Node, opposition North Node, and all square Neptune. Cardinality is action—involvement in a situation and then moving in a new direction. The Node axis indicates relationships, and with Uranus conjunct the South Node there is the probability of sudden changes in relationships. With Neptune squaring the Nodes and Uranus, obstacles or conflicts must be overcome concerning the sudden (Uranus) dissolving (Neptune) of relationships (the Nodes). Neptune in Libra suggests that a partnership relationship could be involved, and the

South Node and Uranus in Cancer would show possible emotionality. The North Node in Capricorn shows that status or security is concerned as well. If one thinks about certain events in her life, there is clear evidence of this complex pattern. Her total involvement with Steven Weed stopped suddenly when her relationship with the Symbionese Liberation Movement began. This relationship was just as strong and suddenly dissolved soon after she was arrested.

The help in this case comes from the Grand Trine in water,* which is connected to the T-Square through Uranus and the South Node. A water Grand Trine signifies strong emotions and compassion, reinforcing points we have already discussed. The specific planets and points are Uranus conjunct South Node, trine Saturn and trine Mercury. The Grand Trine demonstrates emphatically the need for emotional involvement in relationships. Water, however, is also intuitive, and the intuition of this young woman might help her to avoid relationships that show signs of eventually dissolving, especially if she realizes that her emotional needs include structure (Saturn), communications (Mercury) and individuality (Uranus).

With the general picture we have formed of Patricia Hearst, we can now examine any area of her life and, for the most part, see quite clearly how she would feel and behave. This more specific examination will be covered in the next chapter.

---

*See page 43 where exceptions to the specified orbs are given.

Homework Assignment

Patricia Hearst

1. The Sun, Moon and Ascendant comprise the core of the individual. Note the signs these are in, and write a few sentences or a list of key words that might describe Patricia Hearst.

II. With the use of planets, points, signs, houses and aspects, answer the following questions.

A. Patricia Hearst has a need for other people. Give at least three reasons why.

B. What in the chart tells you that she is very emotional? Give at least three reasons.

C. What tells you that she is very adaptable? Give at least three reasons.

6

INTERPRETATION

Homework asssignments.

By reviewing the personality of Patricia Hearst at the beginning of class through the homework assignment, the students are reminded of her general make-up and prepared now to investigate any particular area of her life. The homework assigned at the end of class should deal with an area not covered in class. The total interpretation may take more than one week. In this event the specific area assigned as homework would be discussed at the start of the next class, and the analysis and interpretation continued from there.

Introduction of new materials.

In examining particular areas of the chart, the same approach should be used as was used with the initial examination of the total personality. One would first investigate the general characteristics of an area and then fit the specific parts into this framework in the following manner.

Determine which house (or houses) represent the area to be studied. Some areas are more complex than others and therefore involve more than one house (e.g., the tenth house is career; sixth, daily work; and second, how one earns a living; so together they would describe the employment area). Pages 68-71 may be given to the students to assist them in future interpretations after the process on the following pages has been covered in class.

Note the signs contained in the house or houses. Combine the characteristics of the signs involved in terms of that area. These characteristics provide the basic requirements of the individual in that area.

Since each house represents a number of sub-categories, the student must keep in mind which particular category he is investigating, and direct the interpretation to that specific area. (E.g., the fifth house represents children and love affairs, among other things. If the fifth house contains Capricorn and Aquarius, the interpretation would be as follows: children—one might provide structure and discipline for one's children but expect them to develop as individuals and to have personal freedom as well; love affairs—one is looking for stability and security in a love relationship but also needs to retain his or her individuality, or is attracted to unusual lovers.)

Planets or points (Part of Fortune or Node) positioned within the house being studied add more specific requirements in that area. (E.g., Mercury in the fifth house might mean that communication with children has special importance; or from the viewpoint of love affairs, one is attracted to the mental qualities of a lover.)

If the planets or points in the house are part of a major configuration, describe possible manifestations in that particular area. Previously discussed were general manifestations of the major configurations in terms of the type of aspects, the element of mode and the energies of the planets. Now houses and signs may be added, with the emphasis on the planet in the house.

All other aspects to the planets or points in the house should be combined with the major configurations to expand the total picture. Of particular importance are the hard aspects to the Grand Trines for restraint, and the trines and sextiles to the hard configurations for relief and solutions to problems.

Next, the ruler of the cusp of the house should be located. There is a connection between the house being interpreted and the house in which its ruler is posited. (E.g., if the fifth house has Capricorn on the cusp, and Saturn—the ruler of Capricorn—is in the first house, one's personality might have a strong effect on children or lovers; or one might develop one's personality through children or lovers.)

Aspects to the house ruler will provide even more information about the house being investigated.

Finally, a particular planet or planets associated with some facet of a house might be studied. The sign, house and aspects of the planet might shed more light on the area being investigated. (E.g., Venus and Mars could also be utilized in connection with love affairs, since affection and sex are part of the total relationship.)

There is no set order in which the areas should be examined. One might go around the houses in order and cover all twelve; or one may find that investigation of one area will lead to another, and perhaps only areas of particular interest will be discussed. This, of course, is up to the discretion of the teacher in the classroom situation.

As an example, let us examine love affairs in Patricia Hearst's life. The procedure follows the steps given above.

The house we would look to would be the fifth. Her fifth house contains Capricorn and Aquarius. Therefore she is looking for stability and security in love but also either wishes to retain her individuality, or is looking for an unusual lover (perhaps a revolutionary). The North Node is in the fifth house. Therefore she will probably relate to the world through love relationships. The North Node is involved in a T-Square. It is square Neptune and opposition South Node and Uranus. This configuration was discussed generally in Chapter 5, but the discussion can now be made more specific because one of the points of the T-Square is in the fifth house, and therefore one area in which the possible problem will have to be coped with is the fifth house.

As stated above, Patricia Hearst, with the North Node in the fifth, may relate to the world through love relationships, but there may be sudden changes (Uranus conjunct South Node) or even dissolving (Neptune square the Nodes and Uranus) of a love affair or of other kinds of relationships. Her relationships with her lover (Steven Weed), her friends and her family were dissolved when she joined the Symbionese Liberation Movement. Subsequently, she found a lover in the movement, and then this new love relationship dissolved when her lover was killed.

Besides being involved in the T-Square, the North Node is also semi-square Venus, sextile Mercury, bi-quintile Jupiter, quintile Saturn and trine the MC. The semi-square of Venus indicates that expression of affection might present a problem. The remaining aspects are soft and can be utilized to alleviate this problem. The sextile to Mercury implies that communicating is especially important, and discussion of love problems should be helpful and come about easily. The trine to the MC could mean that creating a favorable public image would lead to alleviation of the relationship problem. The quintile to Saturn shows that she probably gets security from love relationships, and the bi-quintile to Jupiter suggests that love relationships do help her grow and can make her happy, in spite of the possible problems that might be involved. If she were to use the stability of Saturn and the personal expansiveness of Jupiter outside of love relationships, she might not be so dependent on lovers for these attributes. Then the possibility of utilizing the T-Square positively would be more likely. In other words, she might be more independent in her associations and less reliant on the whims of others.

Saturn, the ruler of the fifth house, is in the third, so there is a special connection between communications and love affairs. Since all of the aspects to Saturn are soft, Patricia Hearst probably does derive security quite easily from love relationships, but she may not develop her own inner security and stability because they come so easily from others.

As stated earlier, Venus and Mars (affection and sex) are usually part of love relationships, and they should be examined. Venus is in Pisces, so she can be deeply emotional and self-sacrificing in love. Since Venus is conjunct the Sun, and the Sun is also in Pisces, she might identify her own ego with a lover's; and with Venus in the seventh, the message is repeated. When one considers how she took on the values, ideals, etc. of her lovers and seemed to subordinate her identity to theirs, the manifestation is quite clear. The square from Venus to the MC supports the idea of a possible conflict between her own public image and love or a loved one—in her case this image may have been cast from the lover; the opposition from Venus to the Ascendant shows that there is not only a problem of public image, but also a need to balance (opposition) the lover (Venus) with the way she really is (Ascendant).

The possibility is therefore strong that she will surrender herself totally to a lover. This surrender may restrict her ability to take independent action (square Mars) and to be involved in relationships on her own (semi-square North Node), and it may cause some emotional disturbances (quincunx Moon). The trine from Venus to Saturn, however, indicates that she easily gets security through a lover. The key to helping the problems comes from Saturn because the energy of a trine flows easily. Thus, the love problems could be eventually solved by the trine's helping her to "flow with" this sense of stability and security.

In examining Mars, the expression of sexual urges, we note that it is in the sign of Sagittarius. Hence, the expression of sex can be fairly free, for Mars in Sagittarius of itself does not indicate the personal absorption that Venus in Pisces does. Mars is, however, also connected with the mutable Grand Cross (square Venus and the Sun, opposition MC and square Ascendant). Consequently there is not only a connection between love and sex, but also a connection between them and the problems of image, personality and ego. As with the previous potential difficulties, the possible manifestations should be investigated, along with ways of coping with them.

Examine each area in this way—starting with the general requirements indicated by the characteristics of the signs in the houses, and then relating the planets, planetary signs and aspects to these generalities—so that an integrated view of the area can be formed.

Interpreting a Chart

There are many approaches to interpreting a chart, and the following approach is only one. The emphasis should always be on integrating the chart and visualizing it holistically, rather than concentrating on a single point or aspect.

Step 1. After the chart is erected, a work sheet including both general and specific information would be filled out. All of this material will be included in the interpretation.

Step 2. General qualities and the personality are usually examined first. The following should be included in a discussion of the personality, although not necessarily in this order:
   a. The signs of the Sun, Moon and Ascendant
   b. temperament pattern and hemisphere emphasis
   c. Element and mode emphases by sign and house
   d. Sign emphasis by sign and house
   e. Stelliums (if any)
   f. Planets conjunct the MC and Ascendant (if any)
   g. Characteristics of the signs in the first house
   h. Planets in the first house (if any) and how they are aspected
   i. Ruler(s) of the first house, where it is located and how it is aspected (there could be a co-ruler)
   j. Planet rising before the Sun
   k. Planet last conjuncted by the Moon
   l. Number of planets in positive and negative signs
   m. Mutual reception (if any)
   n. Major configurations discussed generally in terms of the signs, aspects and planets involved.

Step 3. Once the general personality is interpreted, any area of the life may be investigated. Again we start with the general and move to the specific.

    a. Determine which house or houses represent the area to be investigated.

    b. Note the signs contained in the house and combine the characteristics of the signs. These give the basic requirements of the individual in that area.

    c. If there are any planets or points (Node or Part of Fortune) in the house, they will provide more specific requirements in the area.

    d. Then, if the planets or points in the house are connected to a major configuration, the possible expression of the configuration in that area should be discussed.

    e. All other aspects to the planets or points in the house should be integrated with the major configurations for a more complete picture.

    f. Next, locate the ruler of the cusp of the house. There is a connection between the house being interpreted and the house in which its ruler is located.

    g. Note aspects to the house ruler for even more specific information about the house being investigated.

    h. If any particular planet might add to the understanding of the area, the planet's sign, house position and aspects should be added to the total picture. (E.g., Venus, the planet of love, might add information to the house of marriage.)

Some areas that usually seem of interest to the individual, and that would be included in any general interpretation are career, partnerships and the home (origins). There is no specific order in which these areas should be investigated.

Career discussion would include:

1. Signs in the tenth house
2. Planets and points in the tenth house and how they are aspected
3. Planet ruling the tenth house, where it is posited and how it is aspected
4. The sixth house represents daily work, so examining the sixth house in the same manner as the tenth (1-3 above) will provide information supplemental to career requirements
5. The second house represents, among other things, how one earns a living, so it can also supplement the career information
6. Always keep in mind, when investigating any area, the general qualities of the personality because the personality will influence the direction of that area. For instance, if a person needs people you would not tell him to work alone, even if this is a professional possibility.

Partnership discussion would include:

1. Signs in the seventh house
2. Planets and points in the seventh house and how they are aspected.
3. Planet ruling the seventh house, where it is posited and how it is aspected
4. Fifth house if the partnership is a marriage, in the same manner as the seventh (1-3 above) but for courtships
5. Eighth house if the partnership is a marriage in the same manner as the seventh (1-3 above) but for sex and partner's resources
6 Venus (planet of love) for marriage—its house position, sign and aspects will give added information
7. Mars (sexual expression) for marriage—its house position, sign and aspects will give added information

Home discussion would include
1. Signs in the fourth house
2. Planets and points in the fourth house and how they are aspected
3. Planet ruling the fourth house, where it is posited and how it is aspected

The relevant factors for other areas that might be discussed are:

Communications—Third and ninth houses, Mercury and Jupiter

Finances—second house (own resources and earning capacity) and eighth house (others' resources, inheritance)

Health—sixth house (physical health) and twelfth house (mental health)

Social Interaction—eleventh house (group participation) and seventh house (close one-to-one relations), location by sign and house of the Nodes and aspects to them

Children—fifth house for one's children generally and specifically one's first child, seventh for the second child, ninth, the third, etc

7

REINFORCEMENT

Once the basics that were presented in Chapters 1 through 6 have been taught, the next step is to reinforce these materials and to expand the student's understanding by having the student interpret chart after chart. The amount of time required to apply the principles effectively varies, and the approaches to this process are numerous.

It should be stressed that the more knowledge one has of the individual being investigated, the more specific one can be; and that it is not cheating to read about the lives of famous people or to ask questions of known individuals whose charts are being interpreted. Important also, however, is the inclusion of charts of unidentified persons to show how the principles of astrology work and to help the student gain confidence in his or her interpretive ability. In the latter case the teacher should act as the client to steer the student away from a wrong direction. For instance, in the chart of Babe Ruth there is a heavy ninth house emphasis, and the student might feel he is a literary figure. If this supposition is stated the teacher could say, "That is a possibility, but it is not so in this case. What are other ninth house possibilities?"

Following this chapter there are a number of horoscopes of famous people, with questions accompanying each chart. The questions are designed to teach the student to look for repeated messages in various ways, to concentrate on important factors, to develop a systematic manner of investigating specific areas of the life and to integrate the different parts of astrology (signs, planets, houses and aspects).

Some of the questions require specific answers, whereas others which are more speculative elicit more creativity. The questions may be used in their totality, or easier questions may be given first, while the more difficult ones are saved for later.

Another way in which the charts could be assigned as homework is not to use the questions but to ask the students to be prepared to discuss the general personality of the native. Then in class they would discuss their findings and proceed to interpret other areas.

Several charts should be interpreted as a sequence of group exercises. A single chart is assigned to the entire class and questions are answered at home, with information shared in class. Then each student is given a different chart to work on independently and to present to the class. This is a good point at which to introduce the unidentified chart. The sex of the individual would be told. All the students are given copies of each chart, so that they can follow the interpretation in class. In this way, too, they can interpret each chart at home themselves and see how their impressions compare with those of the person interpreting the chart in class. Astrological reasons for each statement must accompany the interpretation. As stated above, the teacher acts as the client to provide guidance as a real client would do. Students should not be made to feel that they must guess who the individual is, but rather they should know that they are working with principles and not with the specifics. When the individual is identified by the teacher at the end of the interpretation, more specific features may be added.

Besides interpreting charts in class, the students must be encouraged to delineate charts for their friends, to whom they would explain that they are students and require feedback to help them acquire more knowledge. They should be advised to give general interpretations and not try to discuss critical problems, or otherwise undertake serious astrological counseling.

In learning astrology, interpreting many, many charts is the most important activity. It is only through application of the knowledge acquired that one truly begins to understand the art. Each interpretation reinforces what has been learned and offers possibilities for increased understanding. No matter how long one studies the subject of astrology, there are always new and exciting discoveries to be made—whether one is a student or a teacher.

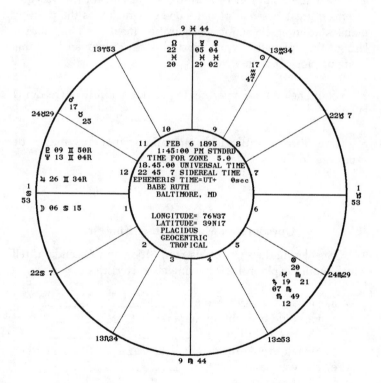

Questions on Babe Ruth

1. Babe Ruth was an individualist. Give two astrological reasons for this statement.

2. He was also a moody person. Give at least two astrological reasons for this assertion.

3. What major configuration might indicate that he had a violent temper which could erupt suddenly?

4. There are a number of astrological reasons for the fact that he was a great baseball player—one of which was the positive manifestation of the major configuration mentioned in 3 above. Using the planets, signs and houses involved in this configuration, explain why.

5. Would he look for a partner to provide stability or freedom? Why?

6. Give three astrological indications that he might be proficient in sports.

Questions on Martin Luther King, Jr.

1. Considering the signs of his Sun, Moon and Ascendant, tell which would explain the following characteristics.

    a. He was conservative. _____
    b. He could be stubborn or persistent. _____
    c. He was ambitious. _____
    d. He felt deeply for people. _____
    e. He was goal-oriented. _____
    f. He "had a dream." _____
    g. He often responded emotionally._____
    h. His resistance was "non-violent." _____

2.   Why would speeches and writing be particularly important in his career?

3.   What indicates that he might find ego satisfaction through religion?

4.   What suggests that he might manifest his creativity through spiritual or religious endeavors?

5.   Using houses, signs and planets, describe why he was involved with equality of groups. Be sure to include astrological reasons for his deep emotional involvement with this cause.

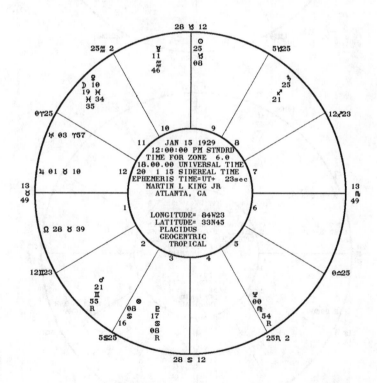

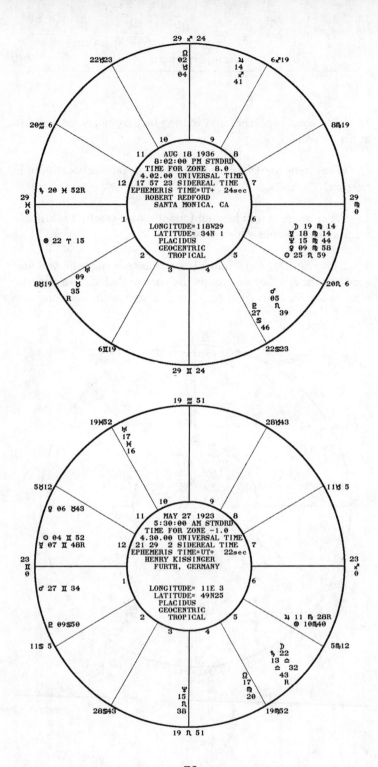

Questions on Robert Redford

1. Consider only the signs of the Sun, Moon and Ascendant, and state which would indicate the following characteristics.

      a.   Acting ability. _____
      b.   Sensitivity to others. _____
      c.   Interest in detail. _____
      d.   Criticalness. _____
      e.   Self-sacrificingness. _____
      f.   "Outgoingness". _____

2. What might tell you that he could have difficulty dealing with abstract ideas?

3. What would tell you that he has traveled a great deal?

4. As a young man, he reportedly was a drifter and drinker. Explain why in terms of a major configuration in his chart. In your explanation use the mode, planets, signs and aspects involved.

5. When he met his wife, his life began to stabilize. This change can be explained as a positive manifestation of the same configuration. Why and how? In your explanation again utilize the mode, planets, signs and aspects.

Questions on Henry Kissinger

1. There are a number of indications that Henry Kissinger's mental qualities are of very special importance. Give three. Your answer should include signs, major configurations and planets.

2. What signs, emphasized in this chart, would show that he might be a good mediator?

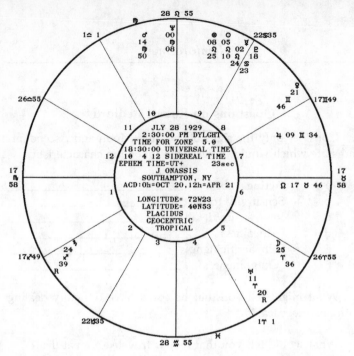

28 ♌ 55

1♎ 1   ♏

♂ 00   ♅   ☊   ☉   ☿   22♋35
14 ♍   00   08 05   ☿
50   08   ♌ ♌ 02   ♇
          25 10 ♌   18
              24/♋
              /23

26♎55

♀
21
♊
46   17♊49

10   9

11   JLY 28 1929   8   ♃ 09 ♊ 34
    2:30:00 PM DYLGHT
    TIME FOR ZONE   5.0
    18:30:00 UNIVERSAL TIME
12   10   4 12 SIDEREAL TIME   7
    EPHEM TIME=UT+   23sec

17   ♏   J ONASSIS   17   ♉
58   SOUTHAMPTON, NY   58
    ACD:0h=OCT 20,12h=APR 21
    1   6   ☊ 17 ♉ 46

    LONGITUDE= 72W23
    LATITUDE= 40N53
    PLACIDUS
    2   GEOCENTRIC   5
        TROPICAL

24 ♐   3   4   ☽
17♐49   ♐   25   26♈55
39   ♈   36
R

22♑35

♅
11
♈
20
R

1♈ 1

28 ♒ 55

3. What tells you that he is a dynamic, hard-driving person?

4. What major configuration demonstrates that he may be highly emotional?

5. What planet in which house shows that there might be changes in his career?

6. Describe the type of person he might seek as a marriage partner.

Questions on Jacqueline Onassis

1. Using the signs of her Sun, Moon and Ascendant, explain why she tries to avoid publicity, and yet often finds herself the center of attention.

2. What is the astrological evidence of her proficiency in French?

3. What indicates her charisma?

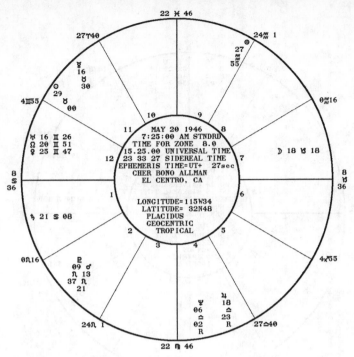

22 ℋ 46

27♈40   24♒ 1
27 ♒ 55

♄ 16 ♉ 30
☉ 29 ♉ 00
4♊55   0♒16

⅄ 16 ♊ 26
☊ 20 ♊ 51
♀ 25 ♊ 47

10   9
11   MAY 20 1946   8
7:25:00 AM STNDRD
15.25.00 UNIVERSAL TIME
23 33 27 SIDEREAL TIME
12   EPHEMERIS TIME=UT+ 27sec   7
CHER BONO ALLMAN
EL CENTRO, CA

LONGITUDE=115W34
LATITUDE= 32N48
PLACIDUS
GEOCENTRIC
TROPICAL

☽ 18 ♑ 18

8 ♋ 36   8 ♑ 36

♅ 21 ♋ 08

1

6

2   5
3   4

0♌16

♇ 09 ♂ ♌ 13
37 ♌ 21

♃ 18 ♎ 23 R
♆ 06 ♎ 02 R   27♎40

24♌ 1

22 ♍ 46

4. What is she looking for in a partner?

5. What are the astrological indications that she could inherit a large amount of money and that this money might come from a partner?

Questions on Cher Bono Allman

1. What are the astrological indications of her musical ability?

2. What would disclose that she might be a basically shy person?

3. Why does she have a strong interdependence with a partner?

4. Using a major configuration in the chart explain the kind of problem that might arise because of this interdependency.

5. How could this problem be alleviated?

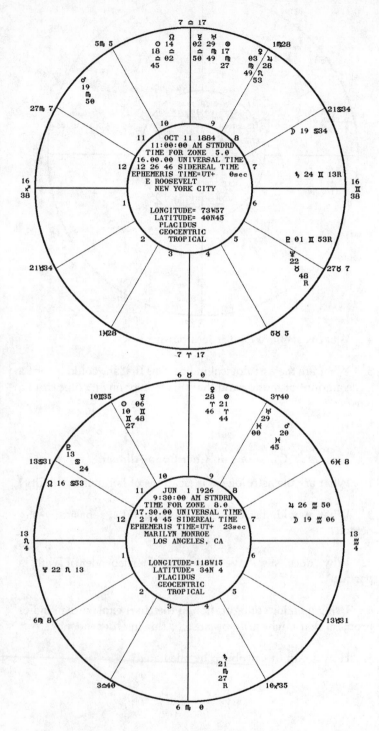

7 ♎ 17

5♏ 5

♌ 14
18 ♎
♎ 02
45

♀ ♅
02 29
♎ ♍ 17
50 49

⊗
♍
27

1♍28

♂
19
♏
50

03 ♃
♍ 28
49 ♌
53

♀

27♏ 7

10   9

11   OCT 11 1884   8
          11:00:00 AM STNDRD
          TIME FOR ZONE 5.0
          16.00.00 UNIVERSAL TIME
12   12 26 46 SIDEREAL TIME   7
          EPHEMERIS TIME=UT+   0sec
          E ROOSEVELT
          NEW YORK CITY

          LONGITUDE= 73W57
          LATITUDE= 40N45
          PLACIDUS
          GEOCENTRIC
          TROPICAL

21♋34

♌ 19 ♋34

♄ 24 ♊ 13R

16
♐
38

16
♊
38

1   6

2   5

3   4

♇ 01 ♊ 53R

♆
22
♉
48
R

27♉ 7

21♑34

1♓28

5♉ 5

7 ♈ 17

---

6 ♉ 0

10♊35

☉ 06
10 ♊
♊ 48
27

♀   ⊗
28 ♈ 21
46 ♈
44

3♈40

♅
29
♓
00   ♂
      20
      45

6♓ 8

♇
13
♋
24

♌ 16 ♋53

10   9

11   JUN 1 1926   8
          9:30:00 AM STNDRD
          TIME FOR ZONE 8.0
          17.30.00 UNIVERSAL TIME
12   2 14 45 SIDEREAL TIME   7
          EPHEMERIS TIME=UT+   23sec
          MARILYN MONROE
          LOS ANGELES, CA

          LONGITUDE= 118W15
          LATITUDE= 34N 4
          PLACIDUS
          GEOCENTRIC
          TROPICAL

13♋31

♃ 26 ♒ 50
☽ 19 ♒ 06

13
♌
4

13
♒
4

♆ 22 ♌ 13

1   6

2   5

3   4

6♍ 8

13♑31

♄
21
♏
27
R

3♎40

10♐35

6 ♍ 0

82

Questions on Eleanor Roosevelt

1. Consider only the signs of the Sun, Moon and Ascendant, and tell which would explain the following characteristics.

      a. Deep feeling in a motherly sense. _____

      b. Outspokenness. _____

      c. Love of distant travel. _____

      d. Home-orientation. _____

      e. Diplomacy. _____

      f. Need for harmony. _____

2. Why would her opportunities usually come from others?

3. What indicates that she developed mainly through experience?

4. She did a great deal of world traveling. Give three astrological reasons.

5. What would indicate that distant travel could be connected with her career?

6. What denotes that writing might also be associated with her career?

Questions on Marilyn Monroe

1. What in Marilyn Monroe's chart indicates that she was called a "sex goddess?"

2. Give five astrological reasons which verify that acting was a good career for her.

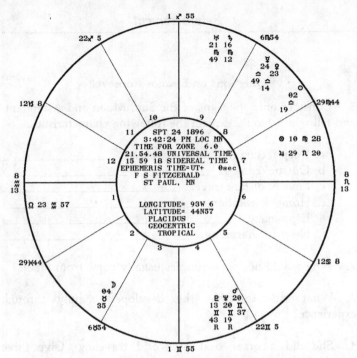

3. What would indicate that her emotions might "run away with her?"

4. What implies that her home was a restrictive area for her?

5. Using a major configuration in the chart, explain what kind of problem she could have had with her mother.

Questions on F. Scott Fitzgerald

1. Consider the signs of the Sun, Moon and Ascendant and tell which would explain the following characteristics.

     a. Individualism. _____
     b. Artistic ability. _____
     c. Need for freedom. _____
     d. Stubbornness. _____
     e. Partnership orientation. _____
     f. Desire to acquire material possessions. _____

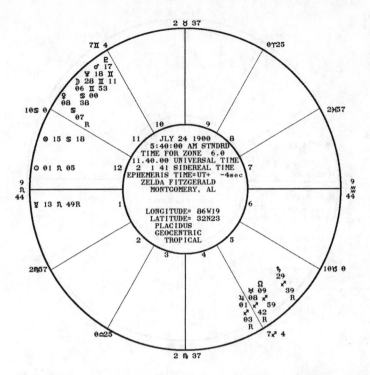

2. What major configuration shows his ability to deal effectively with ideas and abstractions?

3. What major configuration indicates that he might have sudden changes in his relationships?

4. Give at least three astrological indications of his writing ability.

5. Why would distant travel appeal to him?

Questions on Zelda Fitzgerald

1. What indicates that Zelda Fitzgerald needed to balance some parts of her life with other parts?

2. She had an active social life. Give three astrological reasons for this activity.

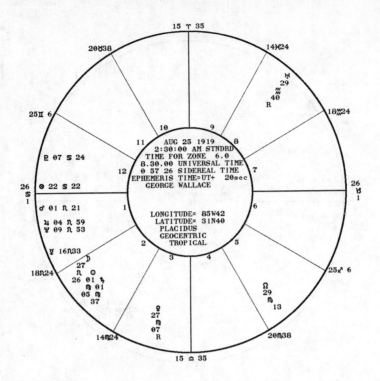

15 ♈ 35

20♉38

14♓24

♅
29
≈
40
R

25♊ 6

18≈24

10   9
11   AUG 25 1919   8
TIME FOR ZONE   6.0
2:30:00 AM STNDRD
8.30.00 UNIVERSAL TIME
12   0 57 26 SIDEREAL TIME   7
EPHEMERIS TIME=UT+   20sec
GEORGE WALLACE

♇ 07 ♋ 24

26
♋
1

⊕ 22 ♋ 22

26
♑
1

1
♂ 01 ♌ 21

6

♃ 04 ♌ 59
♆ 09 ♌ 53

LONGITUDE= 85W42
LATITUDE= 31N40
PLACIDUS
GEOCENTRIC
TROPICAL

☿ 16♌33
☽
2

5
3   4

25♐ 6

18♌24

27
♌ ☉
26 01 ♄
♍ 01
05 ♍
37

☊
29
♍
13

14♍24

♀
27
♍
07
R

20♏38

15 ♎ 35

3. In later life she found great solace in the spiritual. Explain this development astrologically.

4. Why would she feel most comfortable in a large, lavish home?

5. She wrote with an artistic flair and with deep feeling. This endeavor was important to her. Why was this so?

6. What was she looking for in a partner?

Questions on George Wallace

1. Does George Wallace adjust to the world, or does he adjust the world to him? Give the astrological reason.

2. Is he a person of broad or narrow interests? What is the astrological reason?

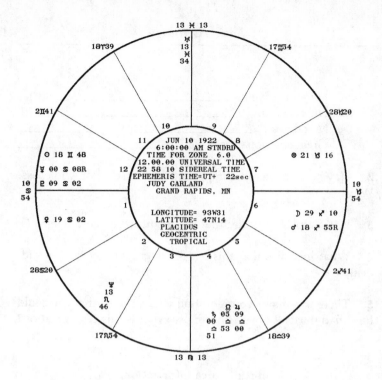

13 ♓ 13
♅ 13 ♓ 34
18♈39
17♒54
2♊41
28♑20
10 9
11 JUN 10 1922 8
6:00:00 AM STNDRD
TIME FOR ZONE 6.0
12.00.00 UNIVERSAL TIME
12 22 58 10 SIDEREAL TIME 7
EPHEMERIS TIME=UT+ 22sec
JUDY GARLAND
GRAND RAPIDS, MN
⊙ 18 ♊ 48
☿ 00 ♋ 08R
⊗ 21 ♑ 16
10 ♋ 54
♇ 09 ♋ 02
LONGITUDE= 93W31
LATITUDE= 47N14
PLACIDUS
GEOCENTRIC
TROPICAL
10 ♑ 54
1 6
♀ 19 ♋ 02
☽ 29 ♐ 10
♂ 18 ♐ 55R
2 5
3 4
28♋20
2♐41
♆ 13 ♌ 46
☊ ♃ ♄ 05 09 ♎ 00 ♎ 53 00 ♎ 51
17♌54
18♎39
13 ♍ 13

3. Give two astrological reasons to explain why he is an initiator.

4. Write a sentence on how each of the planets in his first house might manifest in his personality.

5. Is security important to him? Why or why not?

6. He has been called an effective speaker. Using the third house and Mercury, explain why.

Questions on Judy Garland

1. Consider the signs of the Sun, Moon and Ascendant, and state which would explain the following characteristics.

    a. Outspokenness. _____

    b. Sociability. _____

   c. Love of travel. _____

   d. Nervousness. _____

   e. Moodiness. _____

   f. Great emotionality. _____

2. Having a partner was important for her sense of wholeness. Why?

3. What aspect indicates that she might have had a temper?

4. What indicates that this temper might have flared up suddenly?

5. There is a major configuration which shows that she could have had difficulty in partnerships. What is this configuration?

Birth Source Information

1. Cher Bono Allman: *The Mercury Hour*, April, 1976, p. 48.

2. F. Scott Fitzgerald: Sara Mayfield, *Exiles from Paradise: Zelda and Scott Fitzgerald*, New York: Delacorte Press, 1971, p.29.

3. Zelda Fitzgerald: Ibid, p. 8.

4. Judy Garland: Katherine Clark et al. *Contemporary Sidereal Horoscopes*, San Francisco: Sidereal Research Publications, 1976.

5. Patricia Hearst: Ibid.

6. Martin Luther King, Jr.: William Robert Miller, *Martin Luther King, Jr.*, New York: Weybright and Talley, Inc., 1968, p. 6.

7. Henry Kissinger: *The Mercury Hour*, July, 1975, p. 6.

8. Marilyn Monroe: Stephen Erlewine, *The Circle Book of Charts*, Ann Arbor: Circle Books, 1972, p. 215.

9. Jacqueline Onassis: Marcia Moore and Mark Douglas, *Jacqueline Onassis*, York Maine: Arcane Publications, 1970, p.28.

10. Robert Redford: Katherine Clark et al. op. cit.

11. Eleanor Roosevelt: Archibald MacLeish, *The Eleanor Roosevelt Story*, Boston: Houghton Mifflin, 1965, p. 2.

12. Herman "Babe" Ruth: Gerald Kissinger, "Hank Aaron Makes Baseball History," *Horoscope*, May, 1974, p. 15.

13. George Wallace: Stephen Erlewine, op. cit., p. 186.

All charts were computed by Astro Computing Services, according to the reported birth information given in the sources listed above.

Calculation Form

1. Name: _____

    Source of Data: _____

2. Birthdate: _____

3. Birthplace: _____

    Longitude: _____ Latitude: _____

4. Birthtime (use 24-hour system):

    Daylight Saving Time (if applicable) ___h___ m___ s

    _____ Standard Time ___h___ m___ s

    + *or* − hours from birthplace to
    Greenwich ___h___ m___ s

    −24 if Greenwich Birthtime is over
    24 hours ___h___ m___ s

    Altered Birthdate if Greenwich
    Birthtime is over 24 hours _____

5. Local Sidereal Time:

    Sidereal Time ___h___ m___ s

    + Greenwich Birthtime ___h___ m___ s

    +9.86 seconds × Greenwich
    Birthtime ___h___ m___ s

    = Greenwich Sidereal Time of Birth ___h___ m___ s

    + or − Longitude Time Equivalent
    (E+, W−) ___h___ m___ s

= Local Sidereal Time of Birth   _____h _____m _____s

6.   House Cusps:

Sidereal Time Factor   _____

Latitude Factor   _____

10th (MC)   _____ ° _____ ′

11th   _____ ° _____ ′

12th   _____ ° _____ ′

1st (Asc.)   _____ ° _____ ′

2nd   _____ ° _____ ′

3rd   _____ ° _____ ′

7.   Planets and Points:

Constant:_____

☉ _____	♀ _____	♅ _____
☾ _____	♂ _____	♆ _____
☊ _____	♃ _____	♇ _____
☿ _____	♄ _____	⊗ _____

Interpolation for House Cusps

Placidus house system using hand calculator
and tables of houses from *The American Emphemeris*

Sidereal Time Factor = (Local Sidereal Time − earlier Sidereal Time) ÷ 240

Latitude Factor = minutes of Latitude ÷ 60

Sidereal Time Factor_____Latitude Factor_____

10th House Cusp (MC):

    MC for later Sidereal Time   _____°_____′

    MC for earlier Sidereal Time   _____°_____′

    (Subtract)   (a) _____°_____′

    STF × (a)   = (b) _____

    Earlier MC   _____°_____′

    + (b)   = MC _____°_____′

11th House Cusp:

    11th for later Sidereal Time   _____°_____′

    11th for earlier Sidereal Time   _____°_____′

    (Subtract)   (c) _____°_____′

    STF × (c)   = (d) _____

    Larger house cusp   _____°_____′

    Smaller house cusp   _____°_____′

    (Subtract)   = (e) _____°_____′

    LF × (e)   = (f) _____

    Earlier 11th house cusp   _____°_____′

    + (d)   = _____°_____′

$+$ or $-$ (f) =11th house cusp _____ ° _____ '

12th House Cusp:

    12th for later Sidereal Time   _____ ° _____ '

    12th for earlier Sidereal Time   _____ ° _____ '

    (Subtract)   (g)   _____ ° _____ '

    STF $\times$ (g)   = (h) _____

    Larger house cusp   _____ ° _____ '

    Smaller house cusp   _____ ° _____ '

    (Subtract)   = (i)   _____ ° _____ '

    LF $\times$ (i)   = (j) _____

    Earlier 12th house cusp   _____ ° _____ '

    $+$ (h)   = _____ ° _____ '

    $+$ or $-$ (j). =12th house cusp _____ ° _____ '

1st House Cusp (Asc.):

    1st for later Sidereal Time   _____ ° _____ '

    1st for earlier Sidereal Time   _____ ° _____ '

    (Subtract)   (k)   _____ ° _____ '

    STF $\times$ (k)   = (l) _____

Larger house cusp _____ ° _____ ′

Smaller house cusp _____ ° _____ ′

(Subtract) = (m) _____ ° _____ ′

LF × (m) = (n) _____

Earlier 1st house cusp _____ ° _____ ′

+ (1) = _____ ° _____ ′

+ or − (n) =1st house cusp _____ ° _____ ′

2nd House Cusp

2nd for later Sidereal Time _____ ° _____ ′

2nd for earlier Sidereal Time _____ ° _____ ′

(Subtract) (o) _____ ° _____ ′

STF × (o) = (p) _____ ° _____ ′

Larger house cusp _____ ° _____ ′

Smaller house cusp _____ ° _____ ′

(Subtract) = (q) _____ ° _____ ′

LF × (q) = (r) _____

Earlier 2nd house cusp _____ ° _____ ′

+ (p) = _____ ° _____ ′

+ or − (r) =2nd house cusp _____ ° _____ ′

3rd House Cusp

3rd for later Sidereal Time _____ ° _____ ′

3rd for earlier Sidereal Time _____ ° _____ ′

(Subtract) (s) _____

STF × (s) = (t) _____ ° _____ ′

Larger house cusp _____ ° _____ ′

Smaller house cusp _____ ° _____ ′

(Subtract) = (u) _____ ° _____ ′

LF × (u) = (v) _____

Earlier 3rd house cusp _____ ° _____ ′

+ (t) = _____ ° _____ ′

+ or − (v) =3rd house cusp _____ ° _____ ′

Calculation of Planets

Constant = [(Minutes of Greenwich Birthtime ÷ 60) +Hours of Greenwich Birthtime] ÷ 24

Constant = _____

☉ (Always moves forward)

Position for later date _____ ° ___ ′

Position for earlier date _____ ° ___ ′

Distance traveled _____ ° ___ ′

× Constant = (a) _____

Earlier position _____ ° ′ ″

+ (a) =Birth position ☉ _____ ° ′ ″

☽ (Always moves forward)

Position for later date _____ ° ′ ″

Position for earlier date _____ ° ′ ″

Distance traveled _____ ° ′ ″

× Constant = (b) _____

Earlier position _____ ° ′ ″

+ (b) =Birth position ☽ _____ ° ′ ″

☊ (Always moves backward)

Position for later date _____ ° ___ ′

Position for earlier date _____ ° ___ ′

Distance traveled _____ ° ___ ′

× Constant = (c) _____

Earlier position   _____ ° _____ ′

− (c)   =Birth position ☊ _____ ° _____ ′

☿ (May move forward or backward)

Larger   _____ ° _____ ′

Smaller   _____ ° _____ ′

Distance traveled   _____ ° _____ ′

× Constant   = (d)   _____

Earlier position   _____ ° _____ ′

+ or − (d)   =Birth position ☿ _____ ° _____ ′

♀ (May move forward or backward)

Larger   _____ ° _____ ′

Smaller   _____ ° _____ ′

Distance traveled   _____ ° _____ ′

× Constant   = (e)   _____

Earlier position   _____ ° _____ ′

+ or − (e)   =Birth position ♀ _____ ° _____ ′

♂ (May move forward or backward)

Larger   _____ ° _____ ′

Smaller   _____ ° _____ ′

Distance traveled   _____ ° _____ ′

× Constant   = (f)   _____

Earlier position   _____ ° _____ ′

+ or − (f)　　=Birth position ♂ _____ ° _____ ′

♃　(May move forward or backward)

Larger　　　　　　　　　　_____ ° _____ ′

Smaller　　　　　　　　　　_____ ° _____ ′

Distance traveled　　　　　　_____ ° _____ ′

× Constant　　　　　　= (g)　_____

Earlier position　　　　　　　_____ ° _____ ′

+ or − (g)　　=Birth position ♃ _____ ° _____ ′

♄　(May move forward or backward)

Larger　　　　　　　　　　_____ ° _____ ′

Smaller　　　　　　　　　　_____ ° _____ ′

Distance traveled　　　　　　_____ ° _____ ′

× Constant　　　　　　= (h)　_____

Earlier position　　　　　　　_____ ° _____ ′

+ or − (h)　　=Birth position ♄ _____ ° _____ ′

♅　(May move forward or backward)

Larger　　　　　　　　　　_____ ° _____ ′

Smaller　　　　　　　　　　_____ ° _____ ′

Distance traveled　　　　　　_____ ° _____ ′

× Constant　　　　　　= (i)　_____

Earlier position　　　　　　　_____ ° _____ ′

+ or − (i)　　=Birth position ♅ _____ ° _____ ′

Ψ   (May move forward or backward)

Larger _____ ° _____ ′

Smaller _____ ° _____ ′

Distance traveled _____ ° _____ ′

× Constant   = (j)   _____

Earlier position _____ ° _____ ′

+ or − (j)   =Birth position Ψ _____ ° _____ ′

♀   (May move forward or backward)

Larger _____ ° _____ ′

Smaller _____ ° _____ ′

Distance traveled _____ ° _____ ′

× Constant   = (k)   _____

Earlier position _____ ° _____ ′

+ or − (k)   = Birth position ♀ _____ ° _____ ′

⊗   Part of Fortune (enter signs by number,e.g., Aries, 1; Taurus, 2; etc.)

Ascendant _____ ° _____ ′

+ Moon _____ ° _____ ′

=   _____ ° _____ ′

− Sun _____ ° _____ ′

= Part of Fortune ⊗ _____ ° _____ ′

Placidus Table of Houses for Latitudes 0° to 60° North

3h 44m 0s — 28♉15 — 56° 0' 0"

LAT.	11	12	ASC	2	3
0	26Ⅱ20	24♋6	23Ω41	25♍38	28♎0
5	27 40	26 33	24 53	26 45	27 20
10	27 22	27 46	26 11	26 51	27 20
15	28 22	28 27	26 51	26 53	26 23
20	29 6	29 6	28 18	26 3	26 19
21	29 16	29 17	28 31	26 36	26 36
22	29 25	29 33	28 45	26 32	26 32
23	29 34	0Ω5	28 58	26 23	26 27
24	29 44	0 5	29 11	26 11	26 23
25	29 54	0 21	29 29	26 10	26 19
26	0♋5	0 37	29 38	26 14	26 14
27	0 14	0 10	29 52	26 15	26 10
28	0 24	1 27	0♍6	26 13	26 5
29	0 35	1 27	0 19	26 15	26 1
30	0 46	1 44	0 33	26 16	25 56
31	0 57	2 2	0 57	26 17	25 27
32	1 8	2 19	1 15	26 18	25 22
33	1 20	2 37	2 12	26 21	25 16
34	1 32	2 56	2 41	26 24	25 11
35	1 44	3 14	2 56	26 29	25 5
36	1 57	3 33	3 11	26 34	25 27
37	2 10	3 52	2 12	26 39	25 22
38	2 23	4 12	3 41	26 40	25 16
39	2 37	4 32	4 2	26 42	25 11
40	2 51	4 53	4 58	26 45	24 56
41	3 5	5 14	3 11	26 39	23 54
42	3 21	5 35	4 12	26 42	23 46
43	3 36	5 57	4 41	26 44	23 38
44	3 53	6 20	4 58	26 51	23 30
45	4 10	6 43	5 14	26 11	23 21
46	4 28	7 8	5 56	26 47	23 54
47	4 46	7 31	6 14	26 49	23 46
48	5 6	7 56	6 41	26 51	23 38
49	5 26	8 22	7 58	26 53	23 30
50	5 47	8 49	7 11	27♍0	23 21
51	6 10	9 16	7 30	26 49	23 12
52	6 33	9 45	7 51	26 14	22 53
53	6 58	10 15	8 27	26 18	22 53
54	7 25	10 45	8 33	26 51	22 42
55	7 53	11 16	9 10	27 11	23 21
56	8 24	11 49	7 30	26 49	23 12
57	8 56	12 23	7 51	26 14	22 53
58	9 31	13 0	8 33	27 6	22 53
59	10 9	13 35	8 33	27♍11	22 42
60	10♋50	14Ω13	8♍54	27♍6	22♎32

3h 48m 0s — 29♉13 — 57° 0' 0"

LAT.	11	12	ASC	2	3
0	27Ⅱ15	25Ω5	24Ω42	26♍44	29♎2
5	28 35	27 43	25 54	27 12	28 42
10	28 35	27 28	27 14	28 53	28 22
15	29 17	28 42	28 58	26 58	28 1
20	0Ω56	29 56	29 13	27 27	27 40
21	0 11	0♍12	29 26	27 27	27 36
22	0 20	0 27	29 39	27 27	27 32
23	0 29	0 43	29 52	27 27	27 27
24	0 39	0 59	0♍18	27 27	27 23
25	0 49	1 15	0 18	27 27	27 18
26	0 59	1 31	0 31	27 27	27 14
27	1 9	1 47	0 44	27 27	27 9
28	1 19	2 4	0 58	27 27	27 5
29	1 30	2 20	1 11	27 27	27 0
30	1 41	2 37	1 24	27 27	26 55
31	1 52	2 54	1 38	27 13	26 50
32	2 4	3 12	1 51	27 14	26 46
33	2 15	3 30	2 28	27 15	26 40
34	2 27	3 48	2 19	27 16	26 35
35	2 39	4 6	2 32	27 17	26 30
36	2 51	4 25	2 46	27 18	26 25
37	3 3	4 25	3 1	27 19	26 19
38	3 18	4 47	3 28	27 20	26 14
39	3 31	5 23	3 15	27 21	26 8
40	3 45	5 43	3 44	27 22	26 3
41	4 0	6 25	3 58	27 23	25 57
42	4 15	6 47	4 13	27 24	25 44
43	4 31	6 47	4 28	27 26	25 38
44	4 47	7 32	4 44	27 27	25 32
45	5 4	7 32	4 59	27 28	25 32
46	5 22	7 56	5 15	27 30	25 18
47	5 40	8 45	5 47	27 31	25 11
48	6 0	8 45	6 21	27 32	25 4
49	6 20	9 36	6 21	27 34	24 56
50	6 41	9 36	6 21	27 34	24 56
51	7 3	10 31	6 38	27 35	24 48
52	7 27	10 31	6 56	27 37	24 40
53	7 52	11 30	7 32	27 41	24 32
54	8 18	11 30	7 5	27 41	24 32
55	8 46	12 33	7 55	27 45	24 14
56	9 16	13 41	8 10	27 43	24 5
57	9 49	13 41	8 30	27 46	23 45
58	10 23	14 17	9 10	27 48	23 34
59	11Ω41	14♍55	9♍31	27♎49	23♎23
60	11Ω41	14♍55	9♍31	27♎49	23♎23

3h 52m 0s — 0Ⅱ11 — 58° 0' 0"

LAT.	11	12	ASC	2	3
0	28Ⅱ10	26♋3	25♍44	27♍49	0♍6
5	29 30	28 50	26 54	27 56	29♎45
10	29 24	28 24	27 56	28 24	29 24
15	0♋12	29 37	29 5	28 52	29 2
20	0 57	29 51	0♍8	28 8	28 41
21	1 6	6	0 21	28 6	28 36
22	1 15	1 22	0 33	28 3	28 32
23	1 24	1 37	0 46	28 4	28 27
24	1 34	1 53	0 59	28 4	28 23
25	1 44	2 9	1 10	28 5	28 18
26	1 54	2 24	1 24	28 28	28 13
27	2 4	2 40	1 37	28 28	28 8
28	2 14	2 57	1 50	28 3	28 4
29	2 25	3 13	2 42	28 4	27 59
30	2 36	3 34	2 55	28 5	27 54
31	2 47	3 47	3 35	28 16	27 49
32	2 58	4 4	3 49	28 13	27 44
33	3 10	4 22	4 17	28 14	27 39
34	3 21	4 40	4 31	28 15	27 33
35	3 34	4 58	3 22	28 28	27 28
36	3 46	5 16	3 35	28 16	27 22
37	3 59	5 37	4 45	28 17	27 17
38	4 12	5 59	5 15	28 19	27 11
39	4 26	5 59	5 29	28 19	27 5
40	4 40	6 58	5 44	28 19	26 59
41	4 55	7 20	6 45	28 19	26 53
42	5 10	7 38	6 15	28 20	26 47
43	5 25	7 55	6 31	28 21	26 34
44	5 42	8 13	6 47	28 22	26 34
45	5 58	8 31	7 6	28 23	26 28
46	6 16	8 45	6 15	28 19	26 21
47	6 34	9 33	6 31	28 20	26 13
48	6 54	9 58	6 55	28 21	26 6
49	7 14	10 46	7 17	28 22	25 59
50	7 35	10 24	7 44	28 23	25 51
51	7 57	10 50	8 20	28 24	25 43
52	8 20	11 18	8 38	28 25	25 34
53	8 45	11 51	9 28	28 26	25 26
54	9 11	12 16	9 13	28 27	25 17
55	9 39	12 46	10 8	28 28	25 7
56	10 9	13 18	7 20	28 28	24 58
57	10 41	13 51	7 38	28 25	24 37
58	11 15	14 25	9 28	28 31	24 37
59	11 52	15 0	9 48	28 32	24 26
60	12Ⅱ32	15♍37	10♍8	28♎33	24♎14

3h 56m 0s — 1Ⅱ8 — 59° 0' 0"

LAT.	11	12	ASC	2	3
0	29Ⅱ5	26♋57	26♍47	28♎55	1♍8
5	29 45	29 20	27 54	28 56	0 47
10	0♋25	29 32	28 59	28 58	0 25
15	1 7	0♍32	0♍2	28 59	0 3
20	1 52	1 46	1 46	29 1	29♎41
21	2 1	2 1	1 16	29 3	29 36
22	2 10	2 16	1 28	29 3	29 31
23	2 19	2 31	1 40	29 3	29 27
24	2 29	2 47	1 52	29 3	29 22
25	2 39	3 3	2 3	29 3	29 17
26	2 49	3 18	2 17	29 3	29 12
27	2 59	3 34	2 30	29 3	29 8
28	3 9	3 50	2 42	29 3	28 58
29	3 20	4 6	2 55	29 4	28 53
30	3 30	4 23	3 20	29 4	29 12
31	3 41	4 40	3 33	29 3	29 8
32	3 53	4 57	3 46	29 3	28 42
33	4 3	5 14	3 58	29 4	28 37
34	4 16	5 32	4 11	29 4	28 31
35	4 28	5 50	4 11	29 6	28 26
36	4 41	6 8	4 25	29 4	28 47
37	4 54	6 27	4 38	29 5	28 42
38	4 57	6 46	4 51	29 6	28 37
39	5 14	6 46	5 5	29 6	28 31
40	5 28	7 25	5 19	29 7	28 26
41	5 49	7 45	5 32	29 8	28 47
42	5 59	8 7	5 46	29 8	28 42
43	6 20	8 27	6 15	29 9	28 37
44	6 36	8 48	6 30	29 9	28 31
45	6 53	9 11	6 30	29 9	28 26
46	7 10	9 33	6 45	29 10	28 16
47	7 29	9 57	7 15	29 10	28 9
48	7 48	10 21	7 5	29 10	27 1
49	8 11	10 46	7 47	29 11	26 53
50	8 28	11 12	8 3	29 12	26 45
51	8 51	11 2	8 3	29 12	26 37
52	9 14	12 9	8 19	29 13	26 28
53	9 38	12 44	8 36	29 13	26 10
54	10 32	13 19	8 53	29 14	26 10
55	10 32	13 31	9 11	29 14	26 0
56	11 2	14 3	9 29	29 12	25 50
57	11 33	14 35	10 7	29 13	25 40
58	12 44	15 15	10 25	29 14	25 29
59	12 44	15 43	10 25	29 16	25 18
60	13Ω23	16Ω19	10♍46	29♎16	25♎6

99

FEBRUARY 1954 LONGITUDE

Day	Sid. Time (h m s)	⊙	☽	☽ 12 Hour	Mean Ω	True Ω	☿	♀	♂	♃	♄	⛢	♆	♇
1	8 42 40	11≈ 35 43	7♑ 27 41	14♑ 10 25	23♑ 6	23♑ 59	23≈ 37	12≈ 4	25♏ 2	16Ⅱ 34R	9♏ 7	20♋ 13R	26≏ 3R	24♌ 5R
2	8 46 36	12 36 37	20 59 2	27 53 18	23 0	24 0R	25 20	13 20	25 36	16 32	9 11	20 10	26 3	24 4
3	8 50 33	13 37 31	4≈ 53 0	11≈ 57 47	22 57	23 59	27 3	14 35	26 11	16 30	9 12	20 8	26 3	24 2
4	8 54 29	14 38 23	19 7 57	26 20 30	22 54	23 58	28 45	15 50	26 44	16 29	9 13	20 6	26 3	24 1
5	8 58 26	15 39 15	3✶ 36 49	10✶ 34 23	22 50	23 56	0✶ 25	17 6	27 18	16 28	9 15	20 3	26 2	24 0
6	9 2 23	16 40 4	18 14 12	25 34 23	22 47	23 53	2 3	18 21	27 52	16 27	9 16	20 1	26 2	23 58
7	9 6 19	17 40 53	2♈ 54 12	10♈ 12 51	22 44	23 49	3 38	19 36	28 26	16 26	9 16	19 59	26 2	23 57
8	9 10 16	18 41 40	17 29 36	24 43 50	22 41	23 46	5 11	20 52	29 0	16 26	9 17	19 57	26 1	23 55
9	9 14 12	19 42 26	1♉ 55 55	9♉ 6 47	22 38	23 44	6 41	22 7	29 33	16 25	9 18	19 55	26 1	23 54
10	9 18 9	20 43 10	16 8 49	23 6 20	22 35	23 43D	8 7	23 22	0♐ 7	16 25D	9 19	19 52	26 0	23 52
11	9 22 5	21 43 52	0Ⅱ 43 26	6Ⅱ 55 14	22 31	23 43	9 27	24 37	0 40	16 25	9 20	19 50	26 0	23 51
12	9 26 2	22 44 33	13 8 24	20 27 46	22 28	23 44	10 42	25 52	1 13	16 25	9 21	19 48	25 59	23 49
13	9 29 58	23 45 12	27 8 24	3♋ 45 27	22 25	23 46	11 51	27 8	1 46	16 26	9 21R	19 46	25 59	23 48
14	9 33 55	24 45 49	10♋ 19 5	16 49 28	22 22	23 47R	12 53	28 23	2 20	16 26	9 21	19 44	25 59	23 46
15	9 37 52	25 46 25	6♌ 19 16	29 59	22 19	23 48	13 48	29 38	2 53	16 28	9 21	19 42	25 58	23 45
16	9 41 48	26 47 0	18 36 17	12♌ 21 1	22 16	23 47	14 34	0✶ 53	3 26	16 28	9 20	19 40	25 57	23 43
17	9 45 45	27 47 32	18 47 20	24 48 23	22 12	23 44	15 12	2 8	3 58	16 31	9 20	19 38	25 57	23 42
18	9 49 41	28 48 3	13 16 16	7♍ 9 48	22 9	23 40	15 41	3 23	4 31	16 32	9 19	19 37	25 56	23 40
19	9 53 38	29 48 32	13 22 19	19 22 40	22 6	23 34	16 0	4 38	5 4	16 34	9 18	19 35	25 55	23 39
20	9 57 34	0✶ 49 0	25 27 49	1≏ 14 55	22 3	23 27	16 7R	5 54	5 36	16 36	9 16	19 33	25 55	23 37
21	10 1 31	1 49 27	7≏ 21 29	13 19 1	22 0	23 20	16 5	7 9	6 9	16 38	9 —	19 31	25 54	23 36
22	10 5 27	2 49 52	19 15 35	25 11 33	21 56	23 13	15 53	8 24	6 41	16 41	9 —	19 29	25 53	23 35
23	10 9 24	3 50 15	1♏ 0 6	6♏ 58 8	21 53	23 7	15 32	9 39	7 13	16 43	9 —	19 28	25 52	23 33
24	10 13 21	4 50 37	12 58 9	18 58 8	21 50	23 3	15 1	10 54	7 45	16 46	9 —	19 26	25 51	23 32
25	10 17 17	5 50 58	24 57 37	1♐ 14 35	21 47	23 0D	14 21	12 24	8 17	16 49	9 —	19 25	25 50	23 30
26	10 21 14	6 51 17	7♐ 17 49	13 45 45	21 44	23 0	13 34	13 39	8 49	16 52	9 —	19 23	25 50	23 29
27	10 25 10	7 51 35	19 — —	25 — —	21 41	23 —	12 41	14 —	9 21	16 —	9 —	19 22	25 49	23 27
28	10 29 7	8✶ 51 52	2♑ 9 26	8♑ 38 54	21♑ 41	23♑ 1	11✶ 44	15✶ 54	9♐ 52	16Ⅱ 56	9♏ 15	19♋ 20	25≏ 48	23♌ 26

100

Calculation Form

1. Name: **Patricia Hearst**

   Source of Data: **Contemporary Sidereal**

2. Birthdate: **February 20, 1954**

3. Birthplace: **Berkeley, California**

   Longitude: **122W16** Latitude: **37N52**

4. Birthtime (use 24-hour system):

   Daylight Saving Time (if applicable) ___ h ___ m ___ s

   Pacific ___ Standard Time **18** h **01** m **00** s

   + *or* − hours from birthplace to Greenwich **+8** h ___ m ___ s

   Greenwich Birthtime **26** h **01** m **00** s

   −24 if Greenwich Birthtime is over 24 hours **2** h **01** m **00** s

   Altered Birthdate if Greenwich Birthtime is over 24 hours **Feb. 21, 1954**

5. Local Sidereal Time:

   Sidereal Time **10** h **01** m **31** s

   + Greenwich Birthtime **2** h **01** m **00** s

   +9.86 seconds × Greenwich Birthtime ___ h ___ m **20** s

   = Greenwich Sidereal Time of Birth **12** h **02** m **51** s

+ or − Longitude Time Equivalent
(E+, W−)   **8 h 09 m 04 s**

= Local Sidereal Time of Birth   **3 h 53 m 47 s**

Sidereal Time comes from the ephemeris for the altered birthdate. Greenwich Birthtime comes from 4. above. The multiplication of the Greenwich Birthtime by 9.86 seconds and the addition of the resultant figure to the Greenwich Birthtime converts the clock time to sidereal time. The formula for the hand calculator is: [(minutes of Greenwich Birthtime ÷ 60) + hours of Greenwich Birthtime] × 9.86 seconds. The result is in seconds of time. For Patricia Hearst the Greenwich Birthtime is 2 hours and 1 minute. 1 ÷ 60 = .0167. .0167 + 2 = 2.0167. 2.0167 × 9.86 = 19.8843, so the adjustment, rounded off, to be added to the Greenwich Birthtime is 20 seconds.

To convert longitude into time, 15 degrees of longitude = 1 hour of time; 1 degree of longitude = 4 minutes of time; 1 minute of longitude = 4 seconds of time. Patricia Hearst was born in Berkeley, California: longitude 122w16. 122 ÷ 15 = 8 hours with 2 degrees left over. 2 degrees × 4 minutes = 8 minutes. 16 minutes of longitude × 4 seconds = 64 seconds. The Longitude Time Equivalent, therefore, is 8 hours, 8 minutes and 64 seconds or 8 hours, 9 minutes and 4 seconds.

Since Berkeley, California, is west of Greenwich, the Longitude Time Equivalent is subtracted from the Greenwich Sidereal Time. If Berkeley were east of Greenwich, the Longitude Time Equivalent would be added to the Greenwich Sidereal Time.

When subtracting the Longitude Time Equivalent from the Greenwich Sidereal Time, if the seconds of the Longitude Time Equivalent are greater than the seconds of the Greenwich Sidereal Time, 1 minute must be subtracted from the minutes column of the Greenwich Sidereal Time and added to the seconds column as 60 seconds. If, as is true in this case, the minutes of the Longitude Time Equivalent are greater than the minutes of the Greenwich Sidereal Time, 1 hour must be subtracted from the hours column of the Greenwich Sidereal Time and added to the minutes column as 60 minutes. If the hours of the Longitude Time Equivalent are greater than the hours of the Greenwich Sidereal Time, 24 hours must be added to the hours column of the Greenwich Sidereal Time. (24 hours are just added, without being subtracted from anywhere.) The answer is the local Sidereal Time of Birth.

House Cusps. Two interpolations must be made for houses 11, 12, 1 (Asc.), 2, 3—one for Local Sidereal Time and one for latitude. For the 10th house (MC) only one interpolation must be made, for Local Sidereal Time, because the 10th house is the point due south on the ecliptic (overhead) thus no latitude is involved.

To determine the Sidereal Time Factor turn to the Tables of Houses in the ephemeris, and find the Sidereal Times between which the Local Sidereal Time of Birth falls. The Sidereal Times are given in the upper left-hand corner of each block. They are given in hours, minutes and seconds and are in 4 minute (240 second) intervals. Subtract the smaller Sidereal Time from the Local Sidereal Time. Divide by 240. For Patricia Hearst, Local Sidereal Time of Birth is 3 hours, 53 minutes, 47 seconds. In the Tables of Houses, this time falls between 3 hours, 52 minutes, 00 seconds and 3 hours, 56 minutes, 00 seconds. 3h 53m 47s − 3h 52m 00s = 1m 47s, or 107 seconds. 107 ÷ 240 = .4458, which is Patricia Hearst's Sidereal Time Factor.

To determine the Latitude Factor note the latitude of the birthplace. Divide the minutes of latitude by 60. For Patricia Hearst, latitude of birth is 37ℕ52. 52÷60 = .8667, which is Patricia Hearst's Latitude Factor. Record Sidereal Time Factor and Latitude Factor under 6 on the Calculation Form. All interpolations for Patricia Hearst will be between the Sidereal Times of 3h 52m 00s and 3h 56m 00s and the latitudes of 37° and 38°.

Interpolating

10th House (MC): Find the distance the MC traveled

from the earlier Sidereal Time to the later Sidereal Time. The middle of the top section of each block in the Table of Houses lists the position of the MC. Subtract the earlier MC from the later MC to get the distance (a). (There's no latitude given since the MC is the same for all latitudes). Multiply the distance (converted into minutes if over 1 degree) by the Sidereal Time Factor and add the result to the earlier MC. The Sidereal Time Factor may be placed in the memory of the calculator. The formula would be Distance × Memory Recall = minutes MC traveled to Local Sidereal Time of Birth (b).

For Patricia Hearst:

10th House Cusp (MC):

MC for later Sidereal Time	♊ 1° 08′
MC for earlier Sidereal Time	♊ 0° 11′
(Subtract) (a)	0° 57′
STF × (a) = (b)	25.4125′
Earlier MC	♊ 0° 11′
+ (b) = MC	♊ 0° 36′

57″ × the Sidereal Time Factor or Memory Recall, .4458, = 25.4125. Record next to STF × (a). Earlier MC, 0° 11′, + (b), 25.4125′, = MC, 0° ♊ 36′ rounded off.

If the MC for the earlier Sidereal Time were 29° ♉ 13′ and the MC for the later Sidereal Time were 0° ♊ 11′, a sign or 30° would have to be added to the later MC, so that the subtraction could be done.

As stated previously, there are two interpolations for the 11th, 12th, 1st (Asc.), 2nd and 3rd houses. The procedure for obtaining the Sidereal correction for these houses is the same as for the 10th house. But now we take latitude into consideration. We use the house cusps given for the lower whole degree latitude. (For Patricia Hearst, 37° latitude under 3h 52m 00s and 3h 56m 00s Sidereal Times).

Now write the 11th house cusp given for the later Sidereal Time for the lower whole degree of latitude, and write the 11th house cusp given for the earlier Sidereal Time for the lower whole degree of latitude. Subtract and get (c); multiply by STF or Memory Recall and get (d). Follow the same procedure for the 12th, 1st (Asc.), 2nd and 3rd houses.

For Patricia Hearst:

11th House Cusp:

11th for later Sidereal Time	♋ **4 ° 54** '
11th for earlier Sidereal Time	♋ **3 ° 59** '
(Subtract)	(c)	**0 ° 55** '
STF × (c)	= (d)	**24.5190'**

The lower whole degree of latitude is 37°. The 11th cusp for 37° under the Sidereal Time of 3h 52m 00s is 3° ♋ 59'. The 11th cusp for 37° under the Sidereal Time of 3h 56m 00s is 4° ♋ 54'.

To obtain your Latitude Factor, use the house cusp positions that are given for the two latitudes between which the birth locality latitude falls. Use the positions of the house cusps under the earlier Sidereal Time. By Sidereal Time the house cusps always move forward; by latitude the cusps may move forward or backward. If the house cusp for the later latitude is greater than the house cusp for the earlier latitude, the house cusp is moving forward; if smaller, it is moving backward. Of course 0° of a later sign is larger than 29° of an earlier sign.

Clear the Sidereal Time Factor from the memory, and replace it with the Latitude Factor. Under 11th House Cusp enter the larger house cusp of the two latitudes for the earlier Sidereal Time. Enter the smaller house cusp of the two latitudes for the earlier Sidereal Time. Subtract and get (e); multiply by memory (Latitude Factor). The result is (f) which equals the distance the house cusp moved to birth locality latitude. Write the result in the space after LF × (e) =.

If the house cusp has become larger by latitude, circle +; if it has become smaller, circle −. Add (f) to the house cusp obtained with the sidereal correction if the house cusp has moved forward by latitude; subtract (f) if the house cusp has moved backward by latitude. The result will be the accurate 11th house cusp.

Patricia Hearst's birth latitude is between 37° and 38°. Under 37° for the 11th house we find 3° ♋ 59'. Under 38° for the 11th house we find 4° ♋ 12'. The house cusp is moving forward by latitude, so we circle that + next to (f). We subtract 3°59' from 4°12'. The difference is 13 minutes. 13' × LF, which is .8667 = 11.2667. We add this number to the house cusp with the sidereal correction, and the result is the accurate 11th house cusp.

Larger house cusp	♋ 4 ° 12 '
Smaller house cusp	♋ 3 ° 59 '
(Subtract) = (e)	° 13 '
LF × (e) = (f)	11.2667'
Earlier 11th house cusp	♋ 3 ° 59 '
+ (d) =	♋ 3 ° 83.52'
+ or − (f) = 11th house cusp	♋ 3 ° 95
=	♋ 4° 35'

Follow the same procedure for the other house cusps.

Planets and Points. Planetary positions are given for each day for midnight at Greenwich. One must first determine how much a planet moved from the Greenwich Birthdate to the day after Greenwich Birthdate. The distance is multiplied by the Constant (Greenwich Birthtime ÷ 24), and the result is added to (if the planet is moving forward) or subtracted from (if the planet is moving backward) the position of the planet at 0 hours on the Greenwich Birthdate.

To place the Constant in the memory of the calculator: enter the minutes of the Greenwich Birthtime in the calculator; divide by 60; add the hours of the Greenwich Birthtime, and divide the total by 24. Place the result in the memory, and record the result next to Constant.

Patricia Hearst's Greenwich Birthtime is 2 hours, 1 minute. $1 ÷ 60 + 2 ÷ 24 = .0840$.

The Sun always moves forward, and the position is given in degrees, minutes and seconds. Write the position of the Sun (the Sun column is the second column in the ephemeris) for the day after the Greenwich Birthdate next to Position for later date. Write the Sun position for the Greenwich Birthdate next to Position for earlier date. Subtract. The result will be either minutes and seconds or 1 degree, minutes and seconds. Record next to Distance traveled.

If the result of the initial subtraction is 1 degree, minutes and seconds, convert the 1 degree to 60 minutes, add the 60 minutes to the minutes column and proceed. Enter the seconds of Distance traveled in the calculator, divide by 60 and add this figure to the minutes. Multiply by the Constant. The number to the left of the decimal in the calculator is the minutes to be added to the earlier Sun position. Write that number next to (a) in the minutes column. Subtract the minutes from the calculator and multiply the number to the right of the decimal by 60. The number to the left of the decimal will now be seconds. Write this number next to (a) in the seconds column. Add the minutes and seconds to the earlier Sun position. The result will be the position of the Sun at birth.

Patricia Hearst's Greenwich Birthdate is February 21, 1954. We look at February, 1954 in the ephemeris The Sun's position at 0 hours on February 21, 1954 is 1° ♓ 49′ 27″ and at hours on February 22, 1954 is 2° ♓ 49′ 51″

Constant = **.0840**

☉ (Always moves forward)

Position for later date	♓ 2 °49′51″
Position for earlier date	♓ 1 °49′27″
Distance traveled	1° 0.24″
× Constant = (a)	5′4″
Earlier position	♓ 1°49′27″
+ (a) =Birth position ☉	♓ 1°54′31″

The Moon always moves forward, and the position is given in degrees, minutes and seconds. With the Moon we calculate only the degrees and minutes. If the seconds column is less than 30, use the minutes given in the ephemeris; if 30 or more, add one minute to the minutes column. Subtract the Moon position (column next to the Sun, not "Moon 12 hours") for the Greenwich Birthdate from the Moon position for the day after the Greenwich Birthdate. The answer will be in degrees and minutes. Divide the minutes by 60; add the degrees; multiply by the Constant. The number to the left of the decimal will be the degrees. Write this number next to (b) in the degrees column. Subtract the degrees from the calculator; multiply the remainder by 60. The number to the left of the decimal will be the number of minutes to be added to the earlier Moon position. If the number after the decimal is 5 or more, add 1 minute to the minutes. Write this number next to (b) in the minutes column. Add to the earlier Moon position. The result is the position of the Moon at birth.

☽   (Always moves forward)

Position for later date   ♎ 19° 16'

Position for earlier date   ♎ 7° 21'

Distance traveled   11° 55'

× Constant   = (b)   1°

Earlier position   ♎ 7° 21'

+ (b)   =Birth position ☽   ♎ 8° 21'

The Mean Nodes always move backward; so the position for the later date is always smaller than that for the Greenwich Birthdate. Subtract the later position from the earlier position; multiply the result by the Constant, and subtract the product from the earlier position.

The planets other than the Sun or Moon, may move forward or backward. If the position of the planet for the day *after* the Greenwich Birthdate is smaller than the position for the Greenwich Birthdate, the planet is going backward or is retrograde. The position of the other planets is given in degrees and minutes. Subtract as with the Sun, the Moon and the Nodes; multiply the result by the Constant. Then, add to the Greenwich Birthdate position if the planet is going forward, or subtract from the Greenwich Birthdate position if the planet is going backward.

Mars, Jupiter, Saturn, Uranus, Neptune and Pluto always move a distance of less than a degree. Mercury and Venus usually move more than a degree. If they do move a degree or more, convert the degrees to minutes, and add that number to the minutes before placing them in the calculator. Then multiply by the Constant. The number to the left of the decimal will be the minutes to be added to the earlier position, or subtracted from it if the planet is retrograde.

Since the distance Mars, Jupiter, Saturn, Uranus, Neptune and Pluto travel will always be in minutes (and the distance of Mercury and Venus has already been converted into minutes), there is no division by 60 when the distance is placed in the calculator. Simply enter the number of minutes in the calculator, and multiply by the Constant. As stated above, the number to the left of the decimal will be the number to be added to, or subtracted from, the Greenwich Birthdate position of the planet. If the first number to the right of the decimal is less than 5, record the number of minutes to the left of the decimal; if 5 or more, add 1 minute and record.

For Patricia Hearst, at midnight on February 21, 1954 Venus was at 7^0 ♓ 09′ and at midnight on February 22, at 8^0 ♓ 24′.

♀ (May move forward or backward)

Larger		♓ 8 ° 24 ′
Smaller		♓ 7 ° 09 ′
Distance traveled		1 ° 15 ′
× Constant	= (e)	6.3 ′
Earlier position		♓ 7 ° 09 ′
+ or − (e)	=Birth position ♀	♓ 7 ° 15 ′

The Part of Fortune is Ascendant + Moon − Sun. Write the number of the sign (Aries,1; Taurus,2; etc.), then the degrees and the minutes. When subtracting the Sun , if the minutes of the Sun are larger, borrow 1 degree from the degrees column, and add 60 minutes to the minutes column before subtracting; if the degrees of the Sun are larger, borrow 1 sign, and add 30 degrees to the degrees column; if the number of the Sun's sign is larger, just add 12 signs (do not subtract from anywhere).

For Patricia Hearst:

⊗ Part of Fortune (enter signs by
   number, e.g., Aries, 1; Taurus, 2; etc.)

Ascendant   6 4 ° 23 ′

+ Moon   7 8 ° 22 ′

              = 13 12 ° 45 ′

− Sun   12 1 ° 55 ′

   = Part of Fortune ⊗   1 10 ° 50 ′

              = ♈ 10°50′

ANSWERS TO
HOMEWORK ASSIGNMENTS

Hemisphere Emphasis and Temperament Patterns

A.
1. Splash
2. Seesaw
3. Bundle-Bucket
4. Locomotive

B.
1. 1
2. 3
3. 4
4. 2

C.
1. 2, 3, 4
2. None
3. 1, 4
4. 2, 3

Houses and Planets

A.
1.
  i. physical appearance
  o. the personality
2.
  q. values
  s. one's own earning capacity
3.
  f. short journeys
  u. communications
4.
  j. one's origins

    n. the home
5. r. creative self-expression
    v. children
6. b. physical health
    k. daily work
7. a. open enemies
    d. marriage partners
8. m. other people's money
    w. death
9. c. distant travel
    h. philosophy
10. g. relationship with the outer world
    p. career
11. e. organizations, such as clubs
    t. peer groups
12. l. mental health
    x. institutions

B. ☉ Sun   h. the will
               t. exercise of ego identity
   ☾ Moon   j. the maternal function
               q. responsiveness
   ☿ Mercury   o. lower mind
               s. cleverness
   ♀ Venus   c. love
               n. artistry
   ♂ Mars   m. aggressiveness
               r. initiative
   ♃ Jupiter   d. expansion
               i. optimism
   ♄ Saturn   e. responsibility
               l. frustration
   ♅ Uranus   a. originality
               g. revolutionary activity
   ♆ Neptune   b. spiritualism
               f. illusion
   ♇ Pluto   k. elimination
               p. power

113

C. 1. b. ♂ in 10th house   6.   c. Ψ in 3rd house
    2. c. ♀ in 7th house   7.   b. ♅ in 11th house
    3. a. ♃ in 9th house   8.   c. ☉ in 5th house
    4. a. ♄ in 4th house   9.   a. ☿ in 2nd house
    5. b. ☽ in 1st house   10.   b. ♀ in 6th house

First Six Signs of the Zodiac

A. 1. Virgo ♍   B. 1. Taurus ♉
    2. Gemini ♊   2. Gemini ♊
    3. Leo ♌   3. Leo ♌
    4. Cancer ♋   4. Virgo ♍
    5. Taurus ♉   5. Aries ♈
    6. Aries ♈   6. Cancer ♋

C. 1. aggressive
    2. loyal
    3. fickle
    4. protective
    5. warm
    6. practical

Last Six Signs of the Zodiac

A. 1. Pisces ♓   B. 1. Capricorn ♑
    2. Aquarius ♒   2. Scorpio ♏
    3. Scorpio ♏   3. Pisces ♓
    4. Libra ♎   4. Sagittarius ♐
    5. Capricorn   5. Libra ♎
    6. Sagittarius ♑   6. Aquarius ♒

C. 1. balanced
    2. emotional
    3. fickle
    4. reserved
    5. impersonal
    6. self-sacrificing

Answers

The Signs of the Zodiac

A. 1. Aries ♈ , outgoing
    2. Taurus ♉ , stubborn
    3. Gemini ♊ , sociable
    4. Cancer ♋ , home-loving
    5. Leo ♌ , warm
    6. Virgo ♍ , meticulous
    7. Libra ♎ , balanced
    8. Scorpio ♏ , intense
    9. Sagittarius ♐ , jovial
    10. Capricorn ♑ , conservative
    11. Aquarius ♒ , interested in humanitarian causes
    12. Pisces ♓ , sensitive

B. 1. Aries ♈ , Leo ♌ , Sagittarius ♐
    2. Taurus ♉ , Virgo ♍ , Capricorn ♌
    3. Gemini ♊ , Libra ♎ , Aquarius ♒
    4. Cancer ♋ , Scorpio ♏ , Pisces ♓

C. 1. Aries ♈ , Cancer ♋ , Libra ♎ , Capricorn ♑
    2. Taurus ♉ , Leo ♌ , Scorpio ♏ , Aquarius ♒
    3. Gemini ♊ , Virgo ♍ , Sagittarius ♐ , Pisces ♓

Major Configurations

A. 1. four
    2. three
    3. one
    4. two
    5. six
    6. five

B. 1. six
    2. three
    3. two
    4. one
    5. five
    6. four

After the questions have been answered, the students should be given the names of the individuals from whose charts the configurations have been taken.

1. Muhammad Ali
2. Winston Churchill
3. Christine Jorgensen
4. Jimmy Carter
5. Patricia Hearst
6. Eleanor Roosevelt

Patricia Hearst

I. Sun in Pisces—self-sacrificing; emotional (water); adaptable or fluctuating (mutable); empathetic, compassionate, vulnerable.

Moon in Libra—need for a partner or someone with whom to share, desire for peace and harmony; interest in the mental (air); an ability to act (cardinal) in the interest of another; possible indecisiveness.

Ascendant in Virgo—service-oriented, interest in detail; adaptable or fluctuating (mutable); practical (earth); possibly critical.

The characteristics that would definitely be extremely strong because they are common to all three signs are: interest in and/or dependence upon others; and fluctuation or indecisiveness.

II. A.   Moon in Libra; Sun in Pisces: Virgo Ascendant; Venus in the seventh house; Mercury in the seventh house; etc.

B.   Sun in Pisces; Venus in Pisces; Mercury in Pisces, Grand Trine in Water.

C.   Mutable angles; planets in mutable signs (Sun, Venus and Mercury in Pisces, Jupiter in Gemini, Mars in Sagittarius); planets in mutable houses (Saturn in the third, Sun in the sixth, Pluto in the twelfth.

Babe Ruth

1. Sun in Aquarius; Splay Temperament pattern.
2. Moon in the first house; Ascendant in Cancer; Moon in Cancer; Grand Trine in Water.

116

3. Mars square the Sun, opposition Uranus.
4. This fact can be explained in a number of ways by the Mars in Taurus in the eleventh house, square Sun in Aquarius in the ninth house and opposition Uranus in Scorpio in the fifth house. The fixed T-Square itself shows the ability to pursue and stick to a course taken. The Mars could indicate physical activity before groups (eleventh house). The ego (Sun) would be satisfied through sports (ninth house), by being individualistic (Aquarius). The individuality (Uranus) could also be used creatively (fifth house) for deep emotional satisfaction (Scorpio). Babe Ruth incorporated the physical with sports and expressed it in an individualistic way, which satisfied his ego and his deep emotional needs.
5. Stability. Capricorn in the seventh house with Saturn ruling it.
6. The T-Square may be mentioned again; also Sun in the ninth, Venus in the ninth and Mercury in the ninth.

Martin Luther King, Jr.

1. a. Capricorn Sun
   b. Taurus Ascendant
   c. Capricorn
   d. Pisces Moon
   e. Taurus and Capricorn
   f. Pisces
   g. Pisces
   h. Physical violence is not usually associated with Capricorn, Pisces or Taurus.
2. Mercury in the tenth house.
3. Sun in the ninth house.
4. Neptune in the fifth house, and the ruler of the fifth in the ninth.
5. Aquarius and Pisces in the eleventh house—eleventh house and Aquarius, both indicating causes, and Pisces, emotionality; Moon in Pisces in the eleventh house; the ruler and co-ruler of the eleventh house in water houses.

117

Robert Redford

1.   a. Leo Sun; Pisces Ascendant.
     b. Pisces; Virgo Moon.
     c. Virgo
     d. Virgo
     e. Pisces
     f. Leo
2. No air by sign or house.
3. Jupiter in the ninth house and ruling the ninth.
4. Neptune opposition Saturn in Pisces might indicate the drinking. Venus is pleasure and its being conjunct Neptune could show pleasure in drinking. Neptune conjunct Mercury and the Moon might manifest as confusion in thought and communications (Mercury), which would be emotionally involved or fluctuating (Moon). All these planets are square Jupiter, which could relate to problems with excesses. The opposition of Saturn to Moon, Mercury and Neptune could cause restrictions in his life. The square of Jupiter to Saturn would indicate problems through excesses, involving restriction. The mutable mode suggests the drifting.
5. Partnership might be involved in the expression of this configuration because the ruler of the seventh house (Mercury) is part of the T-Square. The Mutable mode also indicates adaptability. The conjunction of Venus-Neptune-Mercury-Moon could mean finding pleasure through the ideal love, and the ability to express it through the emotions. (Venus is not conjunct Mercury or the Moon, according to the orb of eight degrees given for major configurations. However, Venus is conjunct Neptune, which is conjunct Mercury, which is conjunct the Moon. When there is a multiple conjunction, such as this, I believe the effect is translated from one planet to another.) The opposition from Saturn is the balance of this ideal love with acceptance of responsibility for

others (Pisces). The square from Jupiter signifies personal growth and development through the love and responsibility.

Henry Kissinger

1. Gemini Sun; Gemini Ascendant; Libra Moon; Grand Trine in Air; Gemini emphasis by sign; five planets, Ascendant and MC in air signs; Sagittarius emphasis by house; Mercury conjunct the Sun.
2. The three air signs, especially the Aquarius on the cusp of the house of career.
3. Locomotive Temperament Pattern.
4. Grand Trine in Water.
5. Uranus in the tenth house.
6. With Sagittatius and Capricorn in the seventh house he might look for a partner who is searching for wider horizons, interested in distant travel, etc. (Sagittarius), but who could provide security and prestige and be ambitious (Capricorn). There might be a connection between the partner and work (Jupiter, the ruler of the seventh, is in the sixth). He could even meet the partner through work.

Jacqueline Onassis

1. The Leo Sun might make her the center of attention, and the Aries Moon might push her into the foreground. The Scorpio Ascendant, however, suggests that she desires privacy.
2. Foreign languages are indicated by the ninth house. Mercury is in the ninth and is, among other things, verbal skills. The Sun there indicates the ability to engage wholeheartedly in these skills, and the Part of Fortune there emphasizes again the importance of the ninth.
3. Neptune conjunct MC relates to her charisma. It is

4.   With Taurus on the cusp of the seventh house and
     Gemini in the house as well, she is looking for security
     and communication. Jupiter in the seventh indicates that
     there might be more than one partner. The sextile of
     Jupiter to Mercury again stresses the need for com-
     munication. The ruler of the seventh house, Venus, is in
     the eighth, showing the importance in the partnership
     area of sex and/or the partner's resources. The sextile of
     Venus to the Moon suggests the possibility of emotional
     gratification through the partner, but the opposition to
     Saturn indicates that there might be some restrictions in
     that area, or she might find an older partner.
5.   Pluto in the eighth house implies that she could inherit
     a large amount of money. The ruler of the seventh
     (Venus) in the eighth reveals that the money might come
     from a partner.

also part of a Grand Trine with Saturn and the Moon,
signifying that her charisma emerges easily.

Cher Bono Allman

1.   Indications of her musical ability are Mercury and Sun
     in Taurus, and Venus in the twelfth house.
2.   Saturn in the first house in Cancer.
3.   The ruler of the first house is in the seventh, and the
     ruler of the seventh is in the first. The rulers are also in
     opposition to each other.
4.   The rulers of the first and seventh (Moon and Saturn)
     are in opposition, and both are square Jupiter in the
     fourth house. This cardinal T-Square might indicate
     emotional restrictions in conflict with growth or
     development. Emotional restrictions could lead to
     excesses, or excesses could lead to emotional restrictions.
     Since the planets are in the first, fourth and seventh
     houses, the problems can involve self, home and

partner. Since the rulers of the first and seventh are involved, as well as the first and seventh houses, the possibility of the problem being manifested in connection with the personality and the partner is very strong.

5. With Mercury sextiling the Saturn and trining the Moon, communication is one way of handling the problem directly and fairly easily. With Venus and Uranus trining the Jupiter, the expression of love in an unusual manner is another way of handling the problem.

A very clear manifestation of the problem and its alleviation was her leaving Sonny Bono to marry another man. She continued her career (co-ruler of the tenth house in Jupiter) but discovered that her dependence on Sonny made it difficult for her to perform alone, so she convinced him that they should perform together. This solution to the problem was certainly unusual.

Eleanor Roosevelt

1. a. Cancer Moon
   b. Sagittarius Ascendant
   c. Sagittarius
   d. Cancer
   e. Libra Sun
   f. Libra
1. A majority of her planets are in the western hemisphere.
3. Her Temperament Pattern is a bowl.
4. Sagittarius rising; the ruler of the ninth house in the ninth; Part of Fortune in the ninth.
5. The ruler of the tenth is in the ninth.
6. Writing is also represented by the ninth house, so the answer would be the same as for 5. The ruler of the tenth is in the ninth.

Marilyn Monroe

1. Venus (the planet of female sexuality) is most elevated; Neptune (the planet of idealization or deification) is rising; and they are in trine to each other.
2. Her Ascendant is in Leo; Taurus is on her MC (profession in art); the ruler of the chart is in the tenth house, showing a strong connection between personality and career; Mercury is in the tenth and also in the sign of Gemini—communications are an important part of acting.
3. Grand Trine in Water involving Pluto, North Node, Saturn and Mars. (Pluto is slightly out of orb in its trine to Saturn, but it is "pulled into" the Grand Trine by being conjunct the North Node which is within orb.
4. Saturn in the fourth house.
5. Moon is in opposition to Neptune, and both are square Saturn. Neptune opposition the Moon (mother) might symbolize the disappearing mother, causing restrictions in the home (Saturn in the fourth house square Moon and Neptune).

F. Scott Fitzgerald

1. a. Aquarius Ascendant.
    b. Libra Sun
    c. Aquarius
    d. Taurus Moon
    e. Libra
    f. Taurus
2. Grand Trine in Air including Mercury conjunct Venus, trine the North Node and trine Neptune conjunct Mars.
3. Nodes square Uranus, forming a T-Square.
4. Mercury in Libra; Venus conjunct Mercury; Venus ruling the third house; Moon in Taurus in the third house; Grand Trine in Air.
5. Uranus and Saturn co-rule the chart and are in the ninth house of distant travel.

Zelda Fitzgerald

1. Seesaw Temperament Pattern.
2. Each of the planets in the eleventh house indicates this activity and a comment on each can provide specific information on this area of peers. Pluto represents the power socializing gave her; Mars—enjoyment in being an initiator in the social scene; Neptune—charisma and later drinking acquaintances; Moon—deep emotional involvement; Venus—charm and pleasure in socializing. Also Mercury the ruler of the eleventh, is in the first, showing the importance of her social life to her personality, or vice versa.
3. The spiritual house is the twelfth. With the Part of Fortune there this house is important to her, and there is the possibility of fulfillment for her through the spiritual. The Sun in the twelfth signifies the ability to involve herself wholeheartedly in this area.
4. Jupiter in the fourth house, and trine her Sun.
5. Libra is on the cusp of the third house; Venus, the ruler of the third, is in Cancer and conjunct the Moon. Mercury, the planet of writing, is in the first house—the house of personality.
6. Aquarius on the cusp of the seventh house indicates she was looking for a partner who was an individualist and, perhaps, a humanitarian. With Pisces in the house, she was also looking for deep emotional involvement. The ruller and co-ruler of the seventh house are in the fifth, so having romance in the partnership was also important.

George Wallace

1. He adjusts the world to him because his chart is primarily northern.
2. He is person of narrow interests because his Temperament Pattern is a Bundle-Bucket.

3. His chart is primarily eastern, and Mars is in the first house.
4. Mars would indicate that he is forceful. Jupiter suggests that he is jovial. Neptune could denote that he has charisma or that he is confused about himself. Mercury might mean that he is a talker.
5. Security is important to him because both the lights are in the second house and also because the ruler of the second house is in the second house.
6. The sign Libra and the planet Venus in the third house would give him an artistic flare in his speech-making. Mercury in the first and ruling the third implies that his personality is connected with his speech-making, and Neptune conjunct Mercury could mean that he is charismatic in his speaking.

Judy Garland

1. a. Sagittarius Moon.
   b. Gemini Sun.
   c. Sagittarius.
   d. Gemini.
   e. Cancer Ascendant.
   f. Cancer.
2. She has the Part of Fortune in the seventh house.
3. Mars is in opposition to the Sun.
4. Uranus squares both the Mars and the Sun.
5. The Moon (the ruler of her Ascendant) is opposition Mercury (the ruler of her Sun), and both are square the Nodes (relationships) and Saturn (the ruler of her seventh house).

   It is interesting to note that the four "stars," included in these twelve charts, all have the Moon (emotion) near the cusp of the seventh house (the public) in close opposition or square to Saturn (career), with Mercury (communication) usually involved as well. We see once again how the same aspects can be manifested both negatively and positively.